D0426830

Hierarchy
&
Society

GERALD M. BRITAN *and* RONALD COHEN
editors

Hierarchy
&
Society

ANTHROPOLOGICAL PERSPECTIVES
ON BUREAUCRACY

A Publication of the
Institute for the Study of Human Issues
Philadelphia

Manufactured in the United States of America

Library of Congress Cataloging in Publication Data:

Main entry under title:

Hierarchy and society.

    Includes bibliographies and index.
    CONTENTS: Britan, G. M. and Cohen, R. Introduction.—Britan, G. M. and
Cohen, R. Toward an anthropology of formal organizations.—Nader, L. The
vertical slice: hierarchies and children. [etc.]
    1. Organization—Addresses, essays, lectures. 2. Bureaucracy—Addresses,
essays, lectures. I. Britan, Gerald M. II. Cohen, Ronald. III. Institute for the
Study of Human Issues.
HM131.H514   302.3'5   80-10835
ISBN 0-89727-009-6
ISBN 0-89727-010-X pbk.

For information, write:

Director of Publications
ISHI
3401 Science Center
Philadelphia, Pennsylvania 19104
U.S.A.

Contents

1.

Introduction

GERALD M. BRITAN AND RONALD COHEN

Not many years ago this collection of essays on bureaucracy would have been quite an anomaly. Anthropology's major emphasis was still on simple non–Western cultures, chronicling, analyzing, and theorizing about their "exotic" lifeways. Never mind that the incorporation of small-scale societies into nation-states was becoming one of the most pressing problems of the century. Never mind that anthropology still disguised past history under the awkward label of the "ethnographic present." Never mind that development, urbanization, and the world's increasing economic and political integration had transformed "tribal societies" into ethnic enclaves or imagined reconstructions. Anthropology flourished by excising cultural entities from their national, international, and historical contexts, carving out units of study, partly fictional, partly real, created rather than discovered. The study of these semifictions was our particular sector of the division of labor in social science (see Cohen 1978). Unfortunately, the idea of a world filled with neatly bounded cultural units did not fit the realities of the postcolonial era.

Anthropology's early focus on the study of non–Western lifeways still remains, but today our monopoly, if it ever existed, is gone. Our comparative research, development research, community studies, and other efforts still produce interesting findings, but anthropologists are now joined by scholars from other disciplines, and by natives who demand a strong voice in the description and analysis of their own societies.

As a result, anthropology is now searching for new paradigms and new foci of research. As traditional societies are incorporated into modern industrial states, many anthropologists are turning their attention to the study of complex social systems. To some extent this reflects changing opportunities in employment and foreign fieldwork; it also indicates a growing recognition that anthropologists can add a unique cross-cultural perspective to the understanding and planning of modern life. As they turn from local cultures to large-scale states, however, anthropologists must consider new sets of institutions and must develop the new perspectives and new concepts needed to grapple with them.

Complex societies are just that—complex. Unlike the simpler communities of the past, their identity and character are shaped by many influences. While nearly all facets of a segmentary society can be understood in terms of its lineage system, the integration of a complex industrial society seems in many ways beyond our understanding. History, ideology, economy, family and community, social stratification, polity, and the like have multiple roots and overlapping causes. Thus, adapting anthropological analysis to complex societies involves choices in approach—assumptions about what variables, what sectors of society, provide the most important insights.

Our choice, as editors, rests on what we see as one of the most central, ubiquitous, and powerful elements of complex society: bureaucracy. Bureaucracies are as old as the state itself, and their development has a central place in its evolution, providing a formal structure to administer complex tasks of production, distribution, and governance. Bureaucracies are a crucial link between changing local institutions and the modernizing nations of which they are a part. For complex societies they are a major means through which hierarchical relationships of power and authority are erected and maintained.

Anthropological studies of bureaucracy apply perspectives somewhat different from those already developed in other disciplines. Many writers have taken formal, hierarchical organizations for granted, without asking whether bureaucracies vary in form, function, or process in different social and cultural settings. But the hallmark of anthropology is a comparative and universalistic approach. How do the specific duties of a bureaucracy and its sociocultural context combine to determine its structure? What are the ubiquitous features of formal organization wherever it is found? What is different, similar, or unique about the U.S. Department of Agriculture and its counterpart in Russia, Nigeria, or China? These questions are not new. But while they have always been tangential to the mainstream of organizational theory, they are at the very core of anthropology.

Besides its comparative focus, anthropology has a uniquely strong reliance on ethnographic techniques of data collection. These techniques, used by other disciplines as ancillary devices, focus on how an organization operates in its natural setting, as well as on how it *should* operate and how it is *reported* to operate. We assume that all social contexts may (indeed often do) differ in unknown ways. Thus, we also assume that understanding an organization requires a knowledge of details that may be difficult to identify, even for the organization's members.

Anthropology, therefore, brings to the study of bureaucracy its own traditions of comparative analysis and ethnographic method. How organizational theory will be advanced by these qualities, and how anthropology will be changed by this new subject matter, remain to be seen.

Whatever happens, we are convinced that just as earlier anthropologists analyzed lineages, villages, and age-sets to understand prestate systems, contemporary anthropologists must study bureaucracies and formal organizations to understand the hierarchical relationships of social, economic, and political life within complex states. This need will increase as field research moves from simple, isolated, and often locally autonomous communities to complex social systems of the more and the less developed nations of the world. We must create new models and viewpoints so that anthropology can encompass these new topics while maintaining a holistic and cross-cultural perspective.

This collection of essays is our contribution to an anthropological theory of formal organizations. As in any emerging research area, the essays reflect a varied set of interests, covering topics that range from the nature of non–Western bureaucracies to the dynamics of change in our own government and the increasing bureaucratization of anthropology itself. Yet, despite this variation in empirical focus, a number of common viewpoints clearly emerge.

The essays, first of all, share a belief in the importance of informal organization in formal bureaucratic process. The authors all consider real people who develop the cultural orientations and social practices through which each bureaucracy operates. And they seek to explain how variations within and between bureaucracies reflect broader inter- and intra-cultural differences.

As in more traditional anthropological work, all of the authors describe and interpret what people actually do, the functions they perform, and the interrelations among the hierarchical structures in which they work and live. Because of their tradition of holistic experience in unfamiliar cultures, the anthropologists represented here also tend to look at bureaucracies first from the point of view of participants. Meaning and interpretation are tied closely to the cognitive set of the "natives" rather than to the categories of a deductive schema. Possibly with time we will develop widely applicable general categories. At present, however, bureaucracies must still be seen as exotic and unfamiliar settings whose sociocultural patterns are our first and basic problem.

Many of the essays deal also with policy concerns—how prescriptions and theories for improving social life become translated into organized programs with real consequences, intended and unintended. Some of the essays are concerned with the implications of bureaucratic differences for national development; some focus on how bureaucracies operate as mediating links between larger hierarchies and individual clients; others are concerned with the development and emergence of bureaucracy itself. These all represent important continuing themes for an anthropology of complex societies that incorporates, rather than avoids, an analysis of differences in power and wealth.

The volume opens with the editors' assessment of the place of anthropology in the study of formal organizations. We first consider the relevance of anthropology to the development of the broader, multidisciplinary field of organizational theory. Anthropology, we conclude, provides a holistic framework for integrating formal rules, informal organization, and environmental constraints in the analysis of everyday bureaucratic life. This suggests a number of important research topics: empirical studies of informal organizational dynamics, cross-cultural comparisons of bureaucratic systems, and analyses of the relationship of bureaucracies to their broader social and cultural context. Such research, in our view, will increase the understanding not just of formal organizations but also of more traditional anthropological topics, such as the evolution of the state, the process of social and economic development, and the nature of complex societies.

The volume's substantive essays flesh out this theoretical framework. They begin with Laura Nader's appraisal of a "vertical slice," an analysis of the impact of modern industrial and governmental bureaucracies on children. Nader makes it clear that traditional research on children that remains narrowly focused on the family has become increasingly irrelevant. She documents the manner in which the emergence of industrial society divorced child rearing from the family and home. With example after example, she demonstrates how bureaucracies far removed in space and time—drug companies, food companies, clothing stores, factories, and government agencies—affect the lives of contemporary children. Yet the responsibility of these organizations for the deleterious consequences of their actions is distanced and diluted. Nader clearly feels that changes are needed; that bureaucracies affecting children must be contained and controlled. On a theoretical level, she argues that the modern family is understandable only in relation to the broader hierarchical systems of which it is now a part. We must, in other words, "study up" and consider the larger bureaucratic setting in which much of the control over the lives of our children currently resides.

Following Nader's lead, Helen Schwartzman examines the organizational and bureaucratic context of "Midwest Community Mental Health Center." She focuses on the center's place in a larger hierarchical system that imposes numerous constraints on local action. Schwartzman concludes that state and federal bureaucracies, with their ambiguous and contradictory demands, treat the CMHC as if it were itself a patient in a total institution. This kind of bureaucratic culture, in Schwartzman's view, has a significant effect on the development and dynamics not only of CMHCs, but of a wide range of local service organizations.

In the next chapter, Gerald Britan and Michael Chibnik explore the dynamics of agency relationships within the broader context of the federal government. In analyzing an experimental program of bureaucratic reform, the authors describe informal organizational dynamics in a wide range of federal agencies. Like Schwartzman, Britan and Chibnik discover that agency activities do not merely reflect formal rules or a search for increased efficiency. More important are informal social and cultural groupings and interorganizational relationships. Again, organizational dynamics are understandable only in relation to each agency's place in a larger bureaucratic system and in the larger hierarchy of power that this system reflects.

Ronald Cohen's analysis of "The Blessed Job in Nigeria" takes a similar look at governmental dynamics in a very different sociocultural setting. He clearly demonstrates that bureaucracy is not a constant, but a variable social reality. As in Washington, the Nigerian bureaucracy strongly reflects informal organizational groupings and a broader hierarchical system. Nigeria's bureaucracy, however, is based on informal social organizations and cultural understandings that have led to overcentralized decision making, excessive hierarchy, inexperience, and corruption. Cohen suggests that an "apologist" view of these problems is insufficient. Bureaucracy works differently here not, as some have claimed, because Nigerians are poor at imitating the West or because of the nature of their *traditional* social forms. Instead, Cohen shows that Nigerian bureaucracy has resulted from the legacy of colonialism, postcolonial factionalism, and a lack of efficient monitoring, all of which have been built into its *present* form and culture.

Charles Rosen's analysis of provincial administration in Haile Selassie's Ethiopia further documents how bureaucratic forms can differ and how these differences reflect informal organizations that are part of broader societal processes. Rosen, too, rejects an apologist view of Third World government. His detailed analysis of administrative history in the Ethiopian province of Tegray shows how emerging bureaucratic structures reflect both the development of central authority and the practical realities of local patrimonial systems. His analysis reveals that local bureaucracy cannot simply be imposed; it develops as part of a process of change in which there are continuing nonrational elements. The result in Tegray was a system of administration neither completely modern nor completely traditional. Thus, Rosen's data not only enlighten our understanding of Ethiopian political development, they help to explain the evolution of the modern state itself.

Martin Whyte's examination of "bureaucracy and antibureaucracy" in China provides a broader appraisal of the effect of cross-cultural differences. It also focuses more explicitly on the essential bureaucratic elements of a modern state. Comparing the Soviets and the Chinese, Whyte concludes that, while modern socialist societies may face similar administrative problems, they need not develop similar bureaucratic structures. Differences in the Soviet and Chinese cases, and the strong strain of "antibureaucracy" in China, reflect variations in political ideology and in broader social, cultural, and historical factors. As Whyte sums up, "we should be wary of drawing hard and fast conclusions about the inevitable consequences of bureaucratization. . . . Just as with socialism, there is bureaucracy, and then again there is bureaucracy." There are many inevitable similarities. There are also significant and perhaps predictable differences.

Katherine Newman's study of ostensibly egalitarian workers' collectives in America also aims at the very heart of the bureaucratic structuring of human activities. Does bureaucratic hierarchy result from the nature of tasks and the need to coordinate human efforts in complex activities? Or is it imposed by wider patterns of political and economic stratification? Precisely how much egalitarianism is possible? Newman's findings are thought-provoking. Communal organizations devoted to antihierarchical egalitarianism do tend to become bureaucratized over time. After a close examination of several organizational histories, Newman concludes that this emerging bureaucratic structure reflects each organization's need to interact with other hierarchies that control access to power and wealth. She feels that in a stratified and bureaucratic world the survival of egalitarian collectives requires that they become bureaucracies themselves. Whether or not Newman is ultimately proven right, this is certainly a topic that warrants extensive further research.

The issue is brought forcefully home in the volume's final selection, Bette Denich's analysis of "bureaucratic scholarship." Denich carefully contrasts the diffuse, affective, and personalistic collegial relationships of anthropology's past with an impersonal and bureaucratic present. This reflects not only the growth of numbers in the profession, Denich argues, but also the requirements of hiring, funding, and publication in an increasingly bureaucratized world. Despite the continued expression of a collegial ideal, in Denich's view the bureaucratization of anthropology has had a number of side effects. Today, success for the new professor is highly contingent upon the "ability to rise in the organizational structure of a college or university, invoking the typical methods required for advancement in corporations or in other impersonal organizations. . . ." The new pattern involves highly rationalized criteria for evaluating performance, such as quantity of publication. Similar universalistic criteria govern job placement, student-faculty relations, journal publication, and the like. Whatever its benefits, Denich argues that such bureaucratization has devalued the quality of anthropological scholarship. Perhaps a better balancing of universalistic values and collegial ideals is still possible. For as the earlier papers demonstrate, the structure and content of any bureaucracy are at least potentially variable.

Each selection in this volume offers a significant contribution within its own substantive focus. Many represent the beginning of major new research areas within the discipline. As a whole, moreover, the authors have taken a significant first step toward an anthropology of formal organizations. Certainly, the studies suggest that existing theoretical frameworks are in many ways inadequate. The selections provide new perspectives, raise a number of important new concepts, and supply a substantial body of comparative data. While we cannot yet provide a comprehensive model of bureaucracy, we have indicated the directions future anthropologists can take in developing this important area of inquiry.

Reference

Cohen, Ronald
    1978   Ethnicity: Fashion or Focus in Anthropology. In B. Siegel (ed.), *Annual Review of Anthropology for 1978*. Palo Alto: Annual Review Press.

2.

Toward an Anthropology of Formal Organizations

GERALD M. BRITAN AND RONALD COHEN

The same questions that an earlier generation of anthropologists tackled still give meaning and value to the anthropological quest. Why do people do what they do? How do they group themselves to accomplish those tasks necessary for the (more or less) orderly continuation of social life? How do they understand the world around them? How do their lifeways change, develop, and evolve?

Today, the context of human social life has changed drastically. As local communities have become incorporated into large systems, lineages, clans, age-sets, chiefs, and big men have all declined in importance. Simultaneously, classes, ethnic groups, and formal organizations have emerged with increasing significance throughout the world (Warner 1967). Individuals are now affected less by older units such as family, neighbors, or parish and more and more by "faceless bureaucracies."

> In modern states and cities, such bureaucracies contend against each other for resources and seek to increase their size and influence. . . . The individual is governed now . . . by countless and inexplicable rules of the innumerable bureaucracies with which he must deal in order to survive.[1] [Haviland 1974: 566]

Even if this is true, why should anthropologists become involved? Our hallmark, after all, is the study of small-scale societies, recording, analyzing, and theorizing about exotic cultures and lifeways.

This book is devoted to the notion that the study of bureaucracies and formal organizations is increasingly important to the realization of anthropology's traditional goals. In our view, anthropology is not characterized by a particular empirical focus, but rather by a specialized approach to understanding—a concern for social and cultural context. We learn what something is, how it works, why it does what it does, by investigating its systematic and deeply rooted connections to other activities, events, and arrangements. This approach is based on the direct observation of specific human groups. First we must understand locally accepted meanings and significance. Then we can interpret, compare, and theorize about similar phenomena in other cultural settings.

Today, much of social life is governed by formal organizations, and many of the reasons people are what they are and do what they do result from the activities of bureaucratic agencies. Bureaucracies, in other words, are among the most important sectors of modern life. Yet bureaucracies are themselves made up of interacting individuals arranged into particular structured contexts. In this sense they are amenable to anthropological research. Our goal is to demonstrate how important bureaucracies are to anthropology, to show how anthropologists can and do study them, and to develop some new theoretical concepts and categories for an emerging ethnology of formal organizations.

The Background from Organizational Theory

When Max Weber first developed his model of bureaucracy, the realities of modern political and industrial administration were just emerging. To Weber, contemporary bureaucracies provided (ideally at least) the advantages of scientific rationality over the nepotistic and authoritarian character of an earlier patrimonial system. As logically designed social structures, bureaucracies could equitably meet the organizational and administrative needs of complex societies. Their cold, mechanical efficiency was a necessary complement to machine-age technology; they provided precision, speed, and unambiguity, eliminating from official business love, hatred, and all purely emotional elements (Weber 1947).

The Weberian model is by now widely known. Bureaucracies achieve rational efficiency through well-defined formal structures. Each bureaucracy administers its official duties through an explicit hierarchical system. Specified roles and statuses divide necessary work into orderly spheres of professional competence. Bureaucracies are independent of personalities; their leaders' and members' lives do not intrude in the work environment. Candidates are appointed on the basis of technical qualifications and their work roles are defined by a consistent set of abstract rules. Being a bureaucrat is a career, and promotion occurs in a regularized manner.

In today's terminology, Weber's classical view of bureaucracy is a "closed-system model." Like more recent closed-system theorists, Weber assumes that a bureaucracy's output is for the most part determined by its internal structure. He considers factors such as the technical logic of tasks, the delineation of hierarchical roles, the availability of professional expertise, and the use of proper incentives to motivate performance. Such a closed-system perspective is closely linked to the interests of efficient bureaucratic management and forms the basis for an extensive literature in "scientific" administration (Taylor 1911; Gulick and Urwick 1937; Moonay and Reiley 1931; Brech 1957; Allen 1958). However, it is important to note that these approaches, like the Weberian model from which they are ultimately drawn, are concerned only with bureaucracy in a strictly limited sense, viz. the effects of organizational structure and its "rationality" on goal achievement.

Weber realized that his closed and determinative bureaucratic systems were ideal types and that their utility lay in isolating the internal factors that affect a bureaucracy's operation. Weber chose to ignore a number of nonstructural features which also influence an organization's performance. The characteristics of individual bureaucrats, for example, have no place in a model that divorces formal rules from private interests. The bureaucracy's environment—clients, policy-makers, and outside constituencies—is either ignored or treated as depersonalized input. A focus on formal structure provides a simplified perspective that emphasizes bureaucracy's rational efficiency and ignores various sources of irrationality and complication.

After Weber's seminal work, organizational theory radiated in a number of new directions. (See Thompson 1967 for a summary of the literature.) Students of formal organization built on Weber's foundation, but they were far less interested in an ideal model of bureaucratic rationality. Realizing that more goes on within a bureaucracy than would be expected on the basis of formal rules alone, they developed a "neoclassical" view (Scott 1961) that focused on the study of "informal organization"—the everyday activities of organization members. Sociometric and observational techniques isolated patterns of social interaction that occur outside formal roles, delineating subcultural groups that influence individuals through norms, sentiments, cliques, and status seeking. This "informal organization" was viewed as a spontaneous and functional adaptation by human actors to the problems of bureaucratic life (Roethlisberger and Dickson 1939).

Anthropologists played a major role in developing this perspective and their contributions to the field of organizational behavior were quite impressive. W. Lloyd Warner, for example, was a consultant in the classic Hawthorne studies (Roethlisberger and Dickson 1939) and conducted his own research on an industrial strike (Warner and Low 1947). During the early 1940s, a number of studies of informal industrial organization appeared in the anthropological literature (Arensberg 1942; Barnard 1938; Chapple 1941; Davis et al. 1941; Mayo 1940; Richardson 1941; etc.). In 1943, Warner established the Committee on Human Relations in Industry at the University of Chicago. In 1945, Gardner published one of the first textbooks in the field. By 1946, Warner and Gardner had formed Social Research, Inc., an anthropologically oriented management consulting firm.

The anthropological focus on first-hand observation of cultural process had a significant influence on a number of classic organizational studies by nonanthropologists (e.g., Selznick 1949; Blau 1954; Gouldner 1954). Yet the initial promise of this approach was never fully realized. Organizational case studies soon devolved into idiosyncratic descriptions of bureaucratic psychology, conservatism, and leadership. "Informal organization" began to be viewed simply as an irrational input into an otherwise rational system.

By the mid-1950s a new perspective, the "comparative structural" approach, began to dominate organizational theory (Thompson 1961; Pugh et al. 1963; Hall, Haas, and Johnson 1967; Pugh et al. 1968; Blau and Schoenherr 1971). This closed-system perspective recognized that worker psychology, behavior, and culture varied from organization to organization, but deemed this an irrelevant epiphenomenon of more deeply rooted formal differences. Instead of pursuing case studies of organizational dynamics, structural theorists studied abstract variables in large numbers of organizations. They conducted larger and larger correlational studies relating organizational differences to "structural" factors such as type of technology, degree of hierarchy, or scope of administrative span. Organizations were seen as Durkheimian social aggregates, independent of individual will and variation.

Eventually, the inadequacies of this approach became apparent, for it implied that

> researchers must content themselves with items of information that can be readily picked up and that are reasonably objective in character. Thus, while we may be encouraged to find correlations among a number of structural variables, generally correlations are at such a low level that . . . they provide little guidance to the person of action. [Whyte 1978: 134]

Although, over time, researchers turned to larger systems of variables and more general levels of analysis, significant unexplained variance and contradictory findings always remained (see Downs and Mohr 1976). Abstract correlations simply could not comprehend the complexities of organizational dynamics.

By the early 1970s, a new, processually oriented, open-systems approach began to emerge. Organizations were no longer considered mere amalgamations of formal rules; instead, they were characterized by individuals and groups each attempting to achieve their own goals. Organizational dynamics were not the direct outcome of existing formal structure, but a complex result of social patterns, cultural understandings, and exogenous factors outside the organization's control.

Such an open-systems perspective transcends an analysis of rational organizational efficiency. It refocuses attention on variability and adaptive process within organizations and among them. As a result, much recent research has focused on relations of power, control, and competition that develop as organizations and their members try to optimize access to important yet limited resources. "Neoinstitutional" approaches (McNeil 1971; Perrow 1972; Zald 1970), for example, reflect the influence of earlier qualitative studies, concentrating on internal dynamics as organizations adapt to their environment. This viewpoint is complemented by an emerging "French School" (Tourane 1971; Karpic 1972) that focuses on distinct variable domains: interrelationships among an organization's rational operations, its cultural institutions, and its wider socioeconomic context. Also important is a developing neo-Marxist perspective (Braverman 1975; Goldman 1973; Burway 1975). This approach analyzes the place of formal organizations within the broader social and economic structure of modern "class" society, avoiding the polemics of most Marxist political writings.

One aspect of the open-systems perspective is a renewed interest in the dynamics of informal organization. As a result, a number of recent organizational studies have again adopted an anthropological, case-study approach (e.g., Pettigrew 1973; Hill 1976; Kanter 1977). As one of these organizational theorists recently said:

> anthropologists have been one of the few groups of social scientists willing to spend extended periods of time in the field to test their hypotheses. . . . The present research has been guided by a concern for the elaboration of social structure, for social process . . . a further reason for the choice of these [anthropological] methods is the flexibility they offer. [Pettigrew 1973: 54–55]

Just as importantly, an open-systems approach treats bureaucracy simply as a particular means of organizing human groups, a special case of social organization in general. As such, it provides a congenial framework for an anthropology of formal organizations that remains relevant to our discipline's broader interests.

The Anthropology of Formal Organizations

A full-blown anthropological theory of formal organizations is not currently available, nor at this stage of research is it even desirable. The enormous existing literature on organizational theory needs careful digesting and a corpus of anthropological case studies must be developed. These efforts will undoubtedly yield a more robust set of concepts and theories. What we must do now, however, is elucidate the major dimensions of bureaucracy that must be investigated if comparable data and useful theory are to emerge.

In a limited sense, bureaucracies are everything that Weber said they are, and the Weberian approach provides an important starting point for analysis. Bureaucracies are based on a formal structuring of roles aimed at the fulfillment of designated goals, and structural-functional analysis will therefore continue to have an important place in organizational studies.[2] While broader considerations of societal homeostasis have often been tautological and overly teleological, bureaucracies are in fact purposive entities. In such settings, functional equations are both testable and analytic and the achievement of bureaucratic goals, far from being trivial, is often of central concern. Moreover, in a bureaucracy, unlike an entire society, functional relationships can often be rigorously assessed through experimental and quasi-experimental comparisons.

An anthropology of formal organizations must both widen and sharpen this structural-functional focus. It must consider two related domains of social action that go far beyond mere formal rules: the informal social system and the relations between an organization and its environment. It must, in other words, develop a much more finely grounded perspective toward organizational dynamics.

An understanding of how everyday activities, decisions, factions, and relationships actually work within an organization requires an analysis of informal social networks. Inside formal organizations, and often cross-cutting them, are systems of social relations that develop because people have "natural" affinities to others.[3] These can be based on class, sex, education, age, common interests, or whatever. No matter how or why they form, they are always there and affect organizational activity in a major way.

Similarly, both formal and informal organizational systems are affected by outside activities, persons and groups. The achievement of formal goals requires access to those sectors of a society that provide organizational inputs or use designated outputs. Also important are the families and other identity groups of organization members—their political relations, their class interests, their personal contacts for protection, advancement, and patronage. Finally there are the broader relationships between the culture and ideology of the organization and that of other surrounding organizations and the society as a whole.

In developing an anthropological model, we will first consider the nature of formal organization, informal organization, and environmental relations in greater detail. Then we will examine the implications of these variable domains for a more specific methodology of research.

FORMAL ORGANIZATION

The first problem in conceptualizing and studying formal organizations is the delineation of the unit of study. Bureaucracies may be one or more subunits of a larger structure, such as a government agency, or they may be independent organizations. Variation in the degree of incorporation of one organization into others has a major effect on its relations and integration with its environment. Boundaries are envisaged as a combination of "natural" and heuristic qualities determined by the actual degree of separateness and unit autonomy.

Clearly, a bureaucracy is governed by a number of more or less obvious formal variables that determine its basic features as an operating system. These include such factors as the size of the agency; the demographic characteristics of its personnel; the duties and regulations governing each position and office; the relation of all positions to one another; and the formal rules and recognized practices governing recruitment, tenure, pay, and promotions, as well as the sanctions for lack of proper compliance. These formal variables include an organization's goals as laid down by its charter and by the official statements and policies of its leadership. Other, less obvious factors are also included at the level of formal organization: for example, the degree of hierarchy (the number of levels of command), the distribution of offices and power among personnel, and the participation of underlings in higher-level decision making.

Also essential to a full understanding of organizational process is the degree of conflict among the rules, regulations, and sanctions governing an office (damned if you do, damned if you don't), and the degree of ambiguity in rules and goals. In this vein, we assume that there is a variable degree of discretionary power associated with each position in a bureaucracy, such that the incumbent has some measure of freedom in deciding how to carry out his duties. How much freedom exists and how it is variably located throughout the organization are important factors in understanding how discipline and flexibility are related to everyday operations. The more disciplined or predictable a bureaucracy is, the more it follows a strictly rational Weberian set of operations.

However, rationality in this sense may also mean the organization is less flexible and less adaptive. Conversely, the greater the degree of un-monitored autonomy and freedom, the greater the possibility of corruption, incompetence, and systemic dysfunction. The dilemma of formal organizations is the need to find a middle ground between the constraints of rational rigidity and the inefficiency of too much autonomy.

Formal organization provides a continuing structure within which other relational systems operate. People are not roles or offices. Personal interests, emotions, affinities, and situations bring them into closer contact than formal duties demand, leading to consultation, friend-ships, and intimacy, as well as to factionalism, competition, and hostility. Formal organization forces people into sets of rule-regulated relationships. Within those relationships, "natural" factors of interest, association, and history produce alignments of cooperation and compe-tition that may parallel formal structure, but are not necessarily congruent with it.

The relationship between formal and informal groupings varies according to the power of the constraints each places over the actions of organization members. Formal rules stipulate authority, task require-ments, and the nature of the game. One subordinate, for example, when asked why he was suggesting an obviously inadequate solution to a complex planning problem, quipped, "Don't ask the monkey; ask the organ grinder!" Informal organization can aid in the fulfillment of formally defined goals, or it can hinder or even subvert their achieve-ment. This depends on the nature of informal organization itself and on the informal goals of organization members. Do subordinates seek to gain power at the expense of those already in authority, or do they support the existing system? Are they trying to gain greater personal access to scarce resources, or are they trying to create means by which the organization can itself survive and thrive in its wider environment? Are formal and informal structures compatible or in conflict?

The overall relationship between formal and informal organization depends on the degree to which decisive power over policies and decisions lies in one sector or the other. Theoretically, this leads to three possibilities: (1) the formal is dominant; (2) formal and informal share dominance; and (3) the informal is dominant. In the formal-dominant organization, the *ruling clique* is clearly at the top. Its members stick together and support one another's policies and programs according to the rules. Groups at upper and lower levels in the hierarchy may relate informally in many ways, but it is difficult to gain access to power except through formal channels. Informal groupings generally accept the formal structure or at the very least do not (or cannot) subvert it. The organization functions pretty much as it is supposed to and success, in terms of both adaptiveness and formal output, is a function of the skills and capabilities of the recognized leadership.

Formal-dominant organizations develop informal political cultures in which there is a high degree of consensus about the value of doing things according to the rules. The formal hierarchy is seen as the major means of achieving formal goals—goals which are also accepted as important personal ends by the actors themselves. As a result, change and stability are primarily a function of the degree of success and the age of the leadership. Should the organization prove unsuccessful, higher-ups may force change, subordinates may withdraw support, or the organization may be broken up or incorporated into another bureaucratic system. When the leadership is approaching retirement, a new ruling clique is required. The transition is often smooth, but latent tensions can transform the nature of formal/informal relations, de pending upon the capacity of the new leaders to create a "team" that can pull together as a continuing unit.

In the more balanced formal-informal bureaucracy, the leadership recognizes that there are powerful and potentially disruptive informal subgroupings. Leaders strive to achieve both formal and informal goals so that subgroups can fulfill at least some of their personal wants and needs through cooperation with the formal organization and its specific output requirements. The structure is fraught with possibilities for internal conflict. Stability is achieved only as the result of (1) power sharing among the groups, (2) acceptance by a significant majority that the structure should go unchallenged, and (3) recognition that internal conflict would decrease everyone's access to resources from the wider bureaucratic and societal environment.

Major changes occur when the balance of factors tending toward equilibrium is altered. If an informal subgroup feels it can take over formal leadership, increase its access to resources, enhance its budgetary allocations, or achieve important informal goals, then conflict and competition will result and will continue until new sets of relations between formal and informal sectors are established. If, on the other hand, decreased resources for the entire organization have an unequal impact on formal and informal subgroup interests, conflict and competition will again result and will continue until a new working consensus emerges.

Possibly the least frequent and the most unstable organizational structure emerges when an informal group achieves dominance above and beyond the formal leadership's authority. For reasons of ideology or power seeking, a particular informal network among officials may under certain circumstances come to dominate: (1) if they form a numerical majority; (2) if they have access to sufficient outside influence; or (3) if they quietly but consistently subvert the operation of the organization to obtain their own objectives. Such a situation occurs, for example, when a new regime or administration alters agency leadership to create new programs which are not supported by the majority of bureaucrats who remain in office.

Change and greater stability can result when an informal subgroup gains or regains control, or when a dissident group fissions off to become a separate agency. The informal organization then surfaces to become a formal organization within the larger bureaucratic system. Whether it surfaces or not, informal organization has a strong and continuing effect on everyday organizational activities and on the relationship of a bureaucracy to its broader environment.

THE ENVIRONMENT

Bureaucracies are living systems. As such they must evolve organizational structures that can cope with internal pressures and tensions among their component parts. This is what we have been discussing so far. More to the point, they must also interact with an environment which, under quite normal circumstances, can propel them toward more or less rapid extinction.

At the level of formal structure, relations between a bureaucracy and outside agencies and persons is generally Weberian; that is to say, governed by rules and regulations that stimulate the duties, obligations, rights, and privileges of the organization and its members. Within these rules, an organization competes with others for scarce resources, marshals support for its demands, and responds to pressures and requirements placed on it by other agencies, political groups, factions, and individuals. Formal responses are given to formal demands and the agency tries as best it can to satisfy requests, or to argue convincingly why demands cannot be met.

Formal demands do change over time. New administrative overseers often informally decide to enforce rules and regulations not previously used, sometimes quite suddenly. New demands can create new obligations that are themselves part of the formal structure governing each person's position. New rules, or the reactivation of old ones, can be used to "shake the place up," change demands, and improve outputs.

Informal relations among an organization, its individual members, and its outside environment are a much more complicated topic, yet such relationships often have a major effect on agency activities and operations. Watergate's "Deep Throat," for example, may have been an unofficial informer, but he helped bring about the fall of a presidential administration. Leaving aside such exceptional situations, organizations must always compete for scarce resources; to do so they must provide services or products that impinge on the perogatives of other organizations and that affect the society at large. An agency exchanges support with persons and groups that can in turn support the agency's own programs and access to resources. Informal arm twisting, influence peddling, salesmanship, and intelligence gathering are all adaptive and legitimate bureaucratic strategies. Scarce resources necessitate that agencies interact with outside groups and persons to maintain and expand their formal functions.

The outside environment also affects formal organizations through each individual member's personal network of relationships. Bureaucrats are not simply depersonalized cogs in an administrative machine; their personal lives unavoidably intrude on the work environment. Each bureaucrat's behavior is influenced by his participation in multiple formal and informal outside groupings—his family, his union, his social club, his political party, and so on.

On a more basic level, broad currents of culture and ideology have a pervasive influence on the bureaucrats they surround. Bureaucracies are staffed by people who have particular backgrounds and beliefs that may or may not be shared by large segments of the outside society. In international organizations, for example, the differences and conflicts among staff and clients from varied cultural backgrounds are readily apparent. But even within a single nation-state, the subcultural or professional experience of staff implies that particular orientations are brought to the job. This can be especially evident when a rapid change in regime yields an altered ideology of recruitment, leadership, and policy.

In long-standing bureaucracies, moreover, agencies often develop their own cultural orientations, goals, rituals, language, and norms. This informal "agency culture" can be one of the strongest constraints on bureaucratic innovation. Such patterns can change over time in response to changing conditions, but are often reinforced by the development of similar orientations at other agencies throughout the bureaucratic system.

All these influences on organizational behavior are readily apparent. Though sometimes undesirable, they remain legitimate so long as the bureaucrat does not use a position for illegal personal or corporate gain. The key variable here is dependability—the degree to which an official behaves in accordance with the rules and regulations governing his office. Of course, total dependability means that the bureaucrat uses no judgment and does everything "according to the book." This is honest, but undiscriminating and often inefficient; it blocks the way of others who seek to get things done more efficiently by "cutting corners." Theorizing about corruption, Banfield (1975) suggests that dependability is a function of the degree to which agents have sole discretion over decisions affecting control over scarce resources, the degree to which the regulations they administer are complex and conflicting, and the degree to which they are monitored in their work. To this we would add the widely commented-upon Third World notion that the extent of ethnic, kinship, and regional identification is a strong predictor of a bureaucrat's willingness to provide both legitimate and illegitimate help to clients. This makes the monitoring of bureaucratic behavior extremely important in the long run (see Cohen, Chap. 6 in this volume). Certainly, as the Knapp report on the New York City Police Department demonstrates, a lack of careful monitoring often leads to corrupt practices.

The most important aspect of the present discussion is the notion that analysis of a bureaucracy involves an entire system, not as it should be but as it is. Bureaucrats are people first, officials in organizational positions second. Thus, it is essential for us to understand how they integrate personal, family, ethnic, professional, and political goals and ambitions with their official roles and duties. Personal and official behaviors may often conflict; if we fail to consider issues such as informal organization and corruption, we replace real people with fictional bureaucratic actors. This is what is wrong with the Weberian model and with other approaches that divorce the structure of a bureaucracy from the people who make it work. It is real and living organizations that must be studied.

A METHODOLOGY FOR ANTHROPOLOGICAL RESEARCH

Anthropology studies bureaucracy much as it does any other social setting. The goal is a holistic view of an organization, its personnel, and the context within which it must operate. The basic method rests on the widely validated assumption that direct field studies provide the best evidence for initial generalizations. At the same time, our previous discussion suggests specific sets of data that will be needed for a comparative understanding of formal organizations. Let us go over these briefly.

1. The Nature of Appropriate Analytic Units.   Many formal organizations are vast, ramifying structures that involve thousands of persons. A first task is to draw up a structural chart of the organization, locating all offices and positions and their relations to one another. A temporal dimension should also be included—a history of the organization and its structural development. For fieldwork purposes, however, an entire organization is often too large a unit for study. Smaller subunits, such as agencies or departments, must be heuristically isolated for analysis, just as more traditional fieldwork chooses a particular community or village for study. Often a named unit, such as the "East Side Social Services Agency," or "Widgett Corporation's Department of Personnel," can be isolated. Still, just as a traditional field-worker may wish to visit several villages in one ethnic unit, so a field-worker in a formal organization may work in several departments, or in several social work agencies, or in several high schools. The unit is the arena in which action is observed and recorded. It may be a part of a larger organization, but it provides the stage on which action and plot unfold.

2. *Formal and Informal Rules.* All organizations have both written and unwritten rules. The written rules can be obtained easily from the legislation, constitution, or operations manual of the organization. The unwritten rules must be obtained from observations and interviews. Unwritten rules may be organization-wide, or they may involve formally or informally delineated subgroups. As already noted, rule conflict, ambiguity, and selective enforcement are important aspects of organizational dynamics, as are the degree of autonomy for officials, the degree of monitoring by superiors, and the degree of dependability of actors. Whereas the unit is the stage, the formal rules (including where, when, and how they are applied) provide the stage settings and the scripts.

3. *Input/Output Functions.* As we study the history of an organization, we must consider its formally planned inputs, their (ideal) processing, and the manner in which outputs are then provided for clients, the public, markets, etc. It is folly to study a cigarette factory without obtaining a working knowledge of how cigarettes are made, in that particular plant and elsewhere. Similarly, it is impossible to understand a social service agency without understanding the nature of the services that it provides.

4. *Everyday Activities.* Once an organization's formal structure, rules, and planned input/output are recorded and understood, research can focus on everyday organizational life. Researchers must examine what happens when the organization is working. What do people

actually do? Where? With whom? How does their work vary from hour to hour, from day to day, and from week to week? Unlike traditional field subjects, formal organizations generate large quantities of written records—logs, calendars, memos, minutes, plans, reports. These must be checked against each other and against observed and recorded behavior, for continuities and discrepancies. This record is the observer's basic account of social life in the organization. Its analysis and comparison with other documentary records and interviews about organizational activity provide the basis for an ethnographic depiction.

5. *Informal Networks.*   Theoretically, a natural system of social relations exists within the formal structuring of the organization. Because we assume that this grouping has very important effects on how the organization decides, plans, and carries out its functions, it is essential to obtain a picture of the informal networks that exist within the formal structure and that cut across other agencies and the wider society. Such a picture involves the analysis of role-set material for at least a representative sample of actors, including data on their personal goals and their attitudes toward their organization and others. The contribution that informal groups make to decisions, the degree of competition among them, and the manner in which they relate to the formal organization is the crux of this data set.

6. *Environmental Relations.*   The basic data on environmental relations are formal input/output functions. However, researchers must also analyze formal and informal social and political linkages; cultural continuities and discontinuities; and the degree of dependability, monitoring, and corruption of personnel to place the organization in its broader context. We should collect information on the general history of policies affecting the organization and on the nature of similar agencies.

Sketching these topics provides only a schematic outline for anthropological research. Analysis must consider all these factors and some others. Most importantly, analysis must depict and isolate the dynamic processes through which an organization emerges and evolves. Such analysis provides a basis for understanding bureaucracies as more general social forms, and it can help elucidate the deeper sources of bureaucratic differences and similarities.

At the same time, the anthropology of formal organizations has important practical applications in policy planning and evaluation. Evaluation research, for example, has traditionally utilized experimental approaches based on quantitative comparisons of program results (e.g., Scriven 1969; Weiss 1972), but this provides little under-standing of why observed results occur, or how programs can be improved. Administrators increasingly realize that an understanding of organization context is an essential part of effective planning. In this regard, anthropological studies of formal organizations can provide an extremely useful source of data and analysis (see Britan 1978a, 1978b).

RESEARCH NEEDS

The first step toward an anthropology of formal organizations is the accumulation of more knowledge about everyday organizational dy-namics in a wide range of bureaucratic settings. As the number of empirical studies increases, theoretical generalizations will emerge. Some of the variations in organizational dynamics reflect differences in formal organizational structure—the nature of goals, technology, work rules, leaders, and the like. Other differences are rooted in specific environmental factors—intercompany competition, legal constraints, union structures, or community settings. But in our view, the nature of informal organization is at least as important a determinant of bureaucratic dynamics as are these, and deserves much closer study.

Every organization is influenced by its social and cultural context. Once the blinders of Western ethnocentrism are removed, cross-cultural comparisons of organizational dynamics can help clarify those aspects of bureaucracy essential to modern society, as opposed to those which are merely the outcome of Western acculturation (cf. Gamst 1977). Thus, the second step toward an anthropology of formal organizations is the analysis and comparison of functioning bureaucracies in foreign cultures.

All bureaucracies share a common function as administrative forms through which hierarchical structure—differences in power and wealth—is erected and maintained. This is just as true in our own society as it is in any other. Thus, an anthropology of formal organizations should also focus on how organizations serve as mech-anisms to enforce, or even to change, a society's wider patterns of social and economic relationships. Such "studying up," in Nader's (1972) seminal terms, provides a means of understanding how bureaucratic processes maintain hierarchy and affect people's everyday lives.

These three foci—empirical studies of informal dynamics, cross-cultural comparisons of organizational differences, and examinations of the broader hierarchical contexts that organizations reflect—do not exhaust the topics that an anthropology of formal organization can consider. They do, however, provide a starting point. More importantly, they provide a basis for the development of new anthropological theories that can grapple more effectively with the problems of industrial and postindustrial civilization.

Organizational Theory and Anthropology

The pervasiveness of contemporary bureaucracies is sufficient reason to study them, but such research also has enormous theoretical significance. Bureaucracies play an important part in many of the broader transformations that anthropologists study. For example, the development of formal hierarchy is not just an epiphenomenon of cultural change; it is, in many ways, the crux of political evolution and of the emergence of the state (see Cohen 1978b).

As a special kind of organizational form, bureaucracies provide a useful testing ground for general social theories. In kinship-based societies, social structure is embedded in cultural understandings which are often poorly defined, difficult to elicit, or controversial. The structure of a bureaucracy, however, is, by definition, formal and explicit. As a result, everyday social process—the behavioral variations that are the basis for social change—can be easily articulated for analysis.

Although the rational Weberian model suggests that all complex societies should have similar sets of bureaucratic functions, a cursory appraisal reveals a more complicated reality. Even within a fairly homogeneous cultural area, like Western Europe, each national bureaucracy has developed its own character and style. While comparisons among bureaucracies in the developing world are in their infancy, the differences are even more striking (for example, consider the studies by Cohen, Rosen, and Whyte in this volume). Such differences may well be harbingers of future conflict and change. Certainly, the day in which we could blithely assume that "modernization" was simply the transfer of Western institutions intact is long over.

Differences among national bureaucracies not only reflect differences in political ideology or in lifeways of elites; they are also relevant to social and cultural change. The policies of developing nations are mediated through a wide range of bureaucratic channels, and local communities are affected by bureaucratic agencies that interpret national goals in terms of their own informal organization and understandings (e.g., Britan 1974, 1980; Rosen, Chap. 7 in this volume). The result is a social, cultural, and political process which translates formal policies into options that are quite different from what either central administrators or community residents would expect.

As Foster (1969) so forcefully notes, modern social change cannot be understood without considering the characteristics of the bureaucracies and nation-states that seek to direct it. Bureaucracies are at least as important a factor in economic development as cash markets or individual entrepreneurs. Yet, despite a few suggestive studies, little is really known about how development policies are actually implemented. This involves the analysis not only of formal hierarchical channels but also of the informal social processes through which bureaucracies actually operate.

Anthropological studies of formal organizations should certainly fit into the developing body of organizational theory. Anthropology can add to this theory a firm grounding in ethnographic fieldwork and a new sensitivity to cross-cultural differences. While the anthropology of formal organizations is still in its infancy, it promises to enhance not only our understanding of bureaucracy, but also our understanding of the social and cultural differences that bureaucracies express.

At the same time, a number of issues new to anthropology are emerging from organizational research. The fact that a Weberian view of bureaucracy is at once valid and inadequate produces insight into an ongoing dilemma. As already noted, the more Weberian—i.e., predictable and rational—a bureaucracy's operations, the less freedom there is for its members. In the real world complete predictability is impossible. Regulations cannot cover all situations and overregulation means red tape, entrenched routine, and maladaptation to organizational and human needs. On the other hand, the greater the degree of unmonitored personal discretion by officials, the greater the likelihood of corruption for personal and/or corporate gain by bureaucratic agents.

If anthropological research into formal organization is to create a self-conscious capability to improve bureaucratic efficiency and humaneness, then some theory and data on this dilemma must be accumulated. What bureaucratic values and structures encompass enough, but not too much discipline, enough, but not too much autonomy? What is needed to give organizations a truly human face?

In this vein, we must also consider bureaucracy's more general effect on the depersonalization of human social life. If, as Jacoby (1973) has suggested, the entire world is becoming increasingly bureaucratized, what will this do to society as a whole? To people who fill increasingly narrower bureaucratic pigeonholes? The concept of alienation may be a Marxian invention, but it can be argued that alienation is not only a function of class society, or of industrialization, but also of bureaucratization. Under capitalism, socialism, or any other political system, a citizen must still succumb to authoritarian control and to the dismemberment of his needs, wants, and options by dozens of organizations, each of which is empowered to deal with only a restricted set of activities.

Elsewhere, one of us (Cohen 1978a) has suggested that organizations which involve the whole person will become more salient in modern society. Thus, as bureaucratization grows, so too, we believe, will the importance of family, kin, neighborhood, and ethnicity. These groupings can be identified with emotionally, holistically, and non-bureaucratically. While Marx was certainly right to sense the importance of alienation, he may have been wrong to tie it only to class struggle, not realizing that alienation could also be opposed by other sociocultural factors that emerge to satisfy the needs created by the bureaucratization of human life.

By our definition, a bureaucracy is a hierarchical organization. The inequalities inherent in such a system of relations run counter to deep ideological, religious, political, and emotional desires for equity and equality among human groups and individuals. The attraction of Marxian and Maoist ideology is rooted in such yearnings, arising from life in a bureaucratized world.

But even if bureaucracy is formal *and* hierarchical, how much hierarchy is necessary? Or is it necessary at all? Can humankind organize social life with built-in egalitarianism so that there are no authoritarian leaders or rulers, only people who participate as organized coequals in decisions at all levels? Or is organization *inherently unequal?* The post-Mao era seems to tell us that inefficiency is the cost of enforced equality and that the maintenance of modern societies requires formal sources of coercion and power. These are not simple questions. At present they tend to be settled ideologically. But somewhere in an anthropology of formal organizations such questions must be raised and discussed as empirical issues, rather than as matters of hope and belief.

Another question, one that most often plagues conservatives rather than leftists or liberals, is the relation of bureaucratization to individual freedom and social evolution. Many people yearn for a time when society was simpler and more open, and they instinctively oppose the growth of formal bureaucracy. But is such a reaction realistic? Can bureaucracy be curtailed? Or is it necessary? Does growth follow inexorably from bureaucracy's own internal and adaptive nature? Furthermore, do we want to halt its expansion? Bureaucracy may erode personal liberty, but it also controls unjust relations in which powerful individuals and groups prey freely on the unprotected.

If cultural evolution is the creation of larger and larger institutional constraints upon individual freedom, then bureaucratization is the most recent and most pervasive manifestation of the process. Yet contemporary cultural evolution is no longer completely blind and unplanned. Researchers and planners must establish which aspects of bureaucratic growth benefit the population as a whole, and which are simply undesirable epiphenomena.

These questions have no easy answers. Yet they are crucial to the future of life in complex societies. The study of bureaucracies is, in effect, the study of the most salient and powerful organizations of the contemporary world. How bureaucracies react to their own problems and to ours determines how we live—indeed, whether we continue to live at all. Like it or not, humankind is being driven into a bureaucratized world whose forms and functions, whose authority and power, must be understood if they are ever to be even partially controlled.

Notes

1. This does not mean that we accept or suggest a progressive decline in the capacity of local institutions to contribute to individual development and social participation. Indeed, how such local institutions react to control and incorporation into larger entities—how, why, and when individuals and groups try to create a more humane face to organized social life—is the more positive side of the Luddite notion of alienation.

2. More broadly, we would also argue that structural-functional analysis has a continuing importance for many other anthropological domains and that those who have sounded its death knell (e.g., Leach 1976) are at the very least premature. There is still much to learn about how human groups operate and evolve, and this must necessarily involve structural-functional appraisals (e.g., Boguslaw 1965; Demerath and Peterson 1967; Gamst 1975). Although past functional analyses have often been tautological, this is not, we feel, an intrinsic fault. We must simply ensure that the relationships we consider are measurable (Vayda and Collins 1969) and that they can be related to a dynamic process of selection (Campbell 1965). Structural-functional analysis is essential to an understanding of cultural evolution, which in our view is at least as important a topic as mythical symbolism, the universals of color terminology, or the meaning of right- and left-handedness.

3. The idea of describing informal organization as a "natural" system inside a formal structure was suggested by Martin Landau in a personal discussion with Ronald Cohen.

References

Allen, L. A.
  1958   *Management and Organization*. New York: McGraw-Hill.
Arensberg, Conrad
  1941   Toward a "Control" System for Industrial Relations. *Applied Anthropology* 1: 54–57.
Banfield, Edward C.
  1975   Corruption as a Feature of Governmental Organization. *Journal of Law and Economics* 18: 587–605.

Barnard, Chester
    1938   *The Functions of the Executive.* Cambridge, Mass.: Harvard University Press.
Blau, P.
    1954   *The Dynamics of Bureaucracy: A Study of Interpersonal Relations in Two Government Agencies.* Chicago: University of Chicago Press.
Blau, Peter M., and W. Richard Schoenherr
    1971   *The Structure of Organizations.* New York: Basic Books.
Boguslaw, Robert
    1965   *The New Utopians.* Englewood Cliffs, N.J.: Prentice-Hall.
Brech, E. F. L.
    1957   *Organization.* London: Longmans, Green.
Britan, Gerald M.
    1974   Fishermen and Workers: The Processes of Stability and Change in a Newfoundland Community. Doctoral dissertation, Columbia University.
    1978a   The Place of Anthropology in Program Evaluation. *Anthropological Quarterly* 51: 119–28.
    1978b   Experimental and Contextual Models of Program Evaluation. *Evaluation and Program Planning* 1: 229–34.
    1980   Migration, Modernization, and Government Policy in a Changing Newfoundland Community. In J. Maiola (ed.), *Modernization in Fishing Industries and Communities.* Greenville, N.C.: East Carolina University Press. (In press.)
Braverman, Harry
    1975   *Labor and Monopoly Capital: The Degradation of Work in the Twentieth Century.* New York: Monthly Review Press.
Burway, Michael
    1975   The Hegemonic Organization of Industrial Work. Paper presented at the annual meetings of the American Sociological Society.
Campbell, Donald T.
    1965   Variation and Selective Retention in Socio-Cultural Evolution. In H. R. Barring, G. I. Blanksten, and R. W. Mack (eds.), *Social Change in Developing Areas.* Cambridge, Mass.: Schenkman.
Chapple, Eliot D.
    1941   Organization Problems in Industry. *Applied Anthropology* 1: 2–9.
Cohen, Ronald
    1978a   Ethnicity: Fashion or Focus in Anthropology. In B. Siegel (ed.), *Annual Review of Anthropology for 1978.* Palo Alto: Annual Review Press.
    1978b   Introduction. In R. Cohen and E. Service (eds.), *Origins of the State: The Anthropology of Political Evolution.* Philadelphia: ISHI.
Davis, Allison W., Burleigh B. Gardner, and Mary R. Gardner
    1941   *Deep South: A Social-Anthropological Study of Caste and Class.* Chicago: University of Chicago Press.
Demerath, N. J., and R. A. Peterson (eds.)
    1967   *System, Change, and Conflict: A Reader on Contemporary Sociological Theory and the Debate over Functionalism.* Glencoe, Ill.: Free Press.
Downs, George W., Jr., and Lawrence Mohr
    1976   Conceptual Issues in the Study of Innovation. *Administrative Science Quarterly* 21: 700–14.

Foster, George
1969   *Applied Anthropology.* Boston: Little, Brown.
Gamst, Frederick C.
1975   Rethinking Leach's Structural Analysis of Color and Instructional Categories in Traffic Control Signals. *American Ethnologist* 2: 271-96.
1977   Industrial Ethnology. *Anthropological Quarterly* 50: 1-8.
Goldman, Daniel R.
1973   Managerial Mobility Motivations and Central Life Interests. *American Sociological Review* 38: 119-26.
Gouldner, Alvin W.
1954   Patterns of Industrial Bureaucracy. Glencoe, Ill.: Free Press.
Gulick, L., and L. Urwick
1937   Papers on the Science of Administration. New York: Institute of Public Administration.
Hall, Richard H., J. Eugene Haas, and Norman J. Johnson
1967   Organizational Size, Complexity, and Formalization. *American Sociological Review* 32: 904-12.
Haviland, W.
1974   *Anthropology.* New York: Holt, Rinehart and Winston.
Hill, Larry B.
1976   *The Model Ombudsman.* Princeton: Princeton University Press.
Jacoby, Henry
1973   *The Bureaucratization of the World.* Berkeley: University of California Press.
Kanter, Rosabeth
1977   *Men and Women of the Corporation.* New York: Basic Books.
Karpic, Lucien
1972   Le Capitalisme technologique. *Sociologie du Travail* 14(1): 2-34.
Leach, Edmund
1976   Social Anthropology: A Natural Science of Society. *Proceedings of the British Academy of Science,* vol. 62. London: Oxford University Press.
Mayo, Elton
1940   *The Human Problems of an Industrial Civilization.* New York: Viking.
McNeil, Ken
1971   The Regeneration of Social Organization. *American Sociological Review* 36: 624-37.
Moonay, J. D., and A. C. Reiley
1931   *Onward Industry.* New York: Harper.
Nader, L.
1972   Up the Anthropologist—Perspectives Gained from Studying Up. In D. Hymes (ed.), *Reinventing Anthropology.* New York: Random House.
Perrow, Charles
1972   *Complex Organizations: A Critical Essay.* Glenview, Ill.: Scott, Foresman.
Pettigrew, Andrew M.
1973   *The Politics of Organizational Decision-Making.* London: Tavistock.

Pugh, D. S., D. J. Hickson, C. R. Hinings, K. M. MacDonald, C. Turner, and
T. Lupton
    1963   A Conceptual Scheme for Organizational Analysis. *Administrative
            Science Quarterly* 8: 289–315.
Pugh, D. S., D. J. Hickson, C. R. Hinings, and C. Turner
    1968   Dimensions of Organization Structure. *Administrative Science
            Quarterly* 13: 65–105.
Richardson, Frederick L. W.
    1941   Community Resettlement in a Depressed Coal Region. *Applied
            Anthropology* 1: 24–53.
Roethlisberger, F. J., and W. J. Dickson
    1939   *Management and the Worker.* Cambridge, Mass.: Harvard Univer-
            sity Press.
Scott, William G.
    1961   Organization Theory: An Overview and an Appraisal. *Journal of the
            Academy of Management* 4: 7–26.
Scriven, M.
    1969   The Methodology of Evaluation. In R. Taylor, R. M. Gagner, and
            M. Scriven (eds.), *Perspectives on Curriculum Development.*
            Chicago: Rand McNally.
Selznick, P.
    1949   *TVA and the Grass Roots.* Berkeley: University of California Press.
Taylor, R. W.
    1911   *Principles of Scientific Management.* New York: Harper.
Thompson, James D.
    1967   *Organizations in Action.* New York: McGraw-Hill.
Thompson, Victor A.
    1961   *Modern Organizations.* New York: Knopf.
Tourane, Alain
    1971   *Post-Industrial Society.* New York: Random House.
Vayda, A. P., and P. W. Collins
    1969   Functional Analysis and Its Aims. *Australian and New Zealand
            Journal of Sociology* 5(2): 153–56.
Warner, W. Lloyd
    1967   *Large-Scale Organizations.* Vol. 1: *The Emergent American Society.*
            New Haven: Yale University Press.
Warner, W. L., and J. Low
    1947   *The Social System of the Modern Factory.* New Haven: Yale
            University Press.
Weber, Max
    1947   *The Theory of Social and Economic Organization.* Glencoe, Ill.:
            Free Press.
Weiss, Carol H.
    1972   *Evaluation Research.* Englewood Cliffs, N.J.: Prentice-Hall.
Whyte, William Foote
    1978   Organizational Behavior Research—Where Do We Go from Here? In
            E. M. Eddy and W. L. Partridge (eds.), *Applied Anthropology in
            America.* New York: Columbia University Press.
Zald, Mayer N.
    1970   *Organizational Change.* Chicago: University of Chicago Press.

3.

The Vertical Slice:
Hierarchies and Children

LAURA NADER

Child rearing in modern societies has been linked, on the one hand, with synchronic studies of the family (Lasch 1977) and, on the other hand, with historical research on the rise of children and youth as distinct social groups (Aries 1962; Bendix 1964; Eisenstadt 1956; Harbison and Myers 1963). In his book *Haven in a Heartless World* (1977), Lasch reviews the role social scientists have played in developing public policies about the family, or at least in supporting the dominant views of their day. Discussing sociological studies of families in the 1920s and 1930s, Lasch is surprised that a "discipline concerned with the study of society so systematically excludes social influences on marriage and the family, preferring instead to lay almost its entire stress on the individual's 'attitudes,' on 'unrealistic expectations,' and on 'cultural lag'" (p. 43). Carle Zimmerman is seen as an exception who refused to treat the family in isolation, and who insisted on relating the decay of the family to the growth of the welfare state and to other phenomena such as social mobility (Zimmerman and Frampton 1935). The picture Lasch paints supports his assertion that social scientists have been biased toward an analysis of the intimate family environment. Himself a historian, Lasch points out that historians, too, have failed to consider how broader public policies have impinged on the family and helped to destroy family life.

Sociological studies of childhood, however, have a different emphasis. Some have investigated the linkages between children and the state (Boli-Bennett and Meyer 1978; Bendix 1964). Other research has considered areas where children have organizationally distinct relations:

31

for example, with the law, the economy, the educational system, and leisure institutions. Some scholars see the development of separate institutional linkages with children as repressive (Aries 1962); others see it as liberating (DeMause 1974). The anthropologist's job is to document the nature of these linkages in order to describe their structure and the dynamic role they play in the lives of children and families.

Anthropologists have already studied child rearing in modern societies in relation to the groups, networks, and personal interactions of a residential community. But studies like the one of Orchard Town (Whiting 1963: 873–1010) must extend beyond the residential community to include the separate institutional linkages and hierarchies that affect child rearing even when they seem hidden or distant, and even if including them as part of a holistic model means that parents will seem to play the role of passive intermediaries. Thus, when we ask the same questions we would ask in smaller societies—who is feeding the children, who is clothing them, who is sheltering them, who is entertaining them, and who is determining their genetic legacy—the answer depends upon what part of the institutional hierarchy we are looking at: the family, McDonald's, or General Foods.

A Nigerian anthropologist, John Ogbu, once remarked that America is probably the only country where children are expected to raise themselves. From another perspective, every major institution in this country can be seen as part of the child-rearing organization. Research into child rearing in modern industrial states therefore brings with it the same kind of challenge that the stateless society brought to anthropologists seeking to understand primitive government.

In this paper, I shall focus on the impact of present institutional arrangements and show how we might begin to understand the complex linkages between children and institutions. To do so, we must first acknowledge the *informal* hierarchies that affect our lives, as well as the recognized bureaucratic hierarchies. A quick glimpse at history will help to make the point.

A Historical Perspective

For decades, social scientists have noted the diminishing functions of the American family. In the early history of this country, families were self-reliant; they were grocery stores, schools, medical clinics, and places of employment all rolled into one. When our country was an agricultural society, family farms predominated, and during the period of home industry that followed, the family remained a viable unit of production as well as of consumption. But with the industrial revolution, many family members began working away from home, and away from each other.

As the nation industrialized, protective laws were enacted that encouraged women to stay home and that removed children from the work force. Both were reduced in economic importance and men became increasingly dependent on wage labor. The family became a unit of consumption, but not of production. The "helping professions" expanded and flourished. The previously self-reliant family became a market for big business and a responsibility of an expanding government. Parents, who earlier had both power and responsibility for their children, found their legal responsibility increasing at a time when their power over the intimate home environment was declining.

Although some social scientists have begun to investigate the effect of this sprawling division of labor on children, such studies have generally been of limited scope. Researchers studying schools, for example, have looked at interaction in the classroom and at training for an industrial society, but few have looked at the effect of school budgets. On the other hand, those who study the work place and its effect on the family (Kanter 1977) or the relation of industrial capitalism to the family (Zaretsky 1976) are raising questions ethnographers should answer by detailed study of the hierarchical relationships between children and the major institutions of our society.

One distinct feature of the modern home is its physical separation from the work place, but there is another kind of separation, too—the separation of loyalties. Work raises questions of loyalties when the goals of business clash with the goals of the family. Such a conflict, for example, has been regularly dramatized for millions of corporate and government workers who must grapple with the question of job relocation. For most company employees, the decision not to move requires either outright resignation or stagnation on the career ladder. Moving has its problems, and is undoubtedly related to an increased incidence of alcoholism, drug addiction, and child abuse, and to the fact that 76 percent of all minor and major tranquilizer drugs are consumed by women in this country. Talented people are continually moving in and out of our towns and cities as corporations relocate executives. Their leadership potential is sabotaged. The relocation of entire industries can deeply affect families and communities for generations (Nader 1978).

The structure of work is particularly important in a society where wage labor is the primary source of income, status, family stability, and future insurance. It is crucial in a society in which most people inherit so little, in which there is no land base, in which the family is organized around "isolated" households, and in which there is an absence of support from extended families, the neighborhood, or child-care facilities. A farming household usually had at least a mother and a father at home, as did a household pursuing home industry. With the development of large-scale industry the family dispersed: the father absented himself first and the mother increasingly followed. The peer group became important. Parent time and child time became discrete.

But what happens to children in modern America is not merely a result of what their parents do. While children have become an economic liability for parents, for industry and the professions and industrial sectors of American society the children are big business. Multinationals like Nestlé market milk substitutes around the world. In addition, they can now profit from the belief that mother's milk is often polluted to dangerous levels.

The historical functions of the family were not removed for altruistic reasons, but rather for economic and political ones (Bendix 1964; Harbison and Myers 1963; Katz 1968). Since the state, the business community, and the professions all have a hand in child rearing, to understand children we must investigate the ways in which they are linked to the social security administration, the courts, the insurance industry, and so on.

The real estate industry, for example, has played an important role in age segregation in the United States. Realtors and housing developers build tracts for young couples and "elephant graveyards" for their grandparents. By denying loans on geographic or racial terms, banks have helped realtors segregate the old from the young, the rich from the poor, and the blacks and browns from the whites. Margaret Mead once noted that America would have very different public policies if grandparents lived next door to their grandchildren. Social scientists, then, must not ignore the connection between the real estate industry and the problem of intergenerational ties. Although the consequences of age segregation may be as great as those of racial segregation, for the most part we have not yet analyzed their institutional sources. If we had studied the impact of housing policies on children, we might have discovered an obvious linkage between age segregation and the problems of alienation, anomie, and our inability to pass on knowledge. American children suffer from little sense of history.

Professionals have also encouraged a separation of generations. Today's children often have a different doctor than their mother or their father. Modern families do not even share the same dentist; there are adults' dentists and children's dentists.

Our historical perspective thus helps us to understand the conditions underlying a rapid shift in structures. A picture of children with few effective ties outside the family changes into a picture of children with organizationally distinct relations with a whole variety of separate institutions. These institutions are structured either to manage children or to affect them in the process of "doing business." The following section on technological impact deals with some of the consequences of these hidden hierarchies.

Technological Impacts on Children

We are becoming increasingly sensitive to the human impact of technologies used in the work place. The Occupational Safety and Health Act of 1970 specified that all workers must be guaranteed a safe and healthy place to work. Occupational health specialists regularly report on the work environment (see, for example, Hricko and Brunt 1977), and many of their findings are relevant to children. Lead, for example, has been shown to cause chromosome aberrations which could affect future offspring; it is also correlated with an increased risk of spontaneous abortions in women and with abnormal sperm production in men. Research has also shown that children of female and male operating-room personnel were more likely candidates for miscarriage and birth defects. Although we know that work environments affect children, some employers fail to consider child impact data. Distancing mechanisms, which conceptually separate policy from impact, are characteristic. In the case of Allied Chemicals, which manufactured a chemical, kepone, that poisoned workers and families in Hopewell, Virginia, during the late 1970s, company policy-making was kept separate from considerations of the policy's effect.

Children are often more at risk than mature organisms. For example, they are more susceptible to air pollution, yet ambient air quality standards for seven major pollutants were based on what healthy adults can tolerate. For some pollutants, such as lead, which has a particularly devastating effect on small children's brains, blood, and kidneys, no standard was set until early 1978. In planning for children's health and safety the most obvious facts have been ignored: that children are nearer to the ground and more active than adults. The concentration of some of the heavier pollutants is greatest at lower levels; yet pollution monitoring stations are set between two and fifteen meters above ground, high above a child's breathing zone. Children's needs are ignored in other areas as well. Many early childhood deaths result from car accidents, yet child restraints (seat belts and harnesses) are not legally mandated. Distancing mechanisms suppress the knowledge that the world of the child suffers from the hands of the adult.

The story of children and industrial organizations continues: childbirth drugs are invented to allow the hospital to run more smoothly and birth defects increase; formula feeding becomes big business and simultaneously malnutrition increases. In spite of sophisticated improvements in medical technology, infant mortality remains high. The food industry now provides Americans with over five pounds of additives a year, most of which have unknown effects (Schroeder 1974). The same industry persuades children to consume sugar, salt, and starch in quantities that are known to be bad for their health. The cigarette ad "You've come a long way, baby" has succeeded in getting more women between twenty and thirty years (heavy childbearing years) to smoke than ever before, and has done so consciously.

The story of Tris, a carcinogenic chemical used in children's pajamas as a flame retardant, reveals government ineptitude and the chemical industry's self-interest. The carcinogenic and sterilizing effect of this chemical has been well documented (Blum and Ames 1977), and the Consumer Product Safety Commission banned Tris. However, a technicality was found and the resultant court challenges set the ban aside, only to have it reimposed soon after. The evidence is still muddy as to the health effects of present retardants.

Over the past several decades, case after case of chemical disaster has caught the attention of the press. In 1962 the world was shocked to learn that Thalidomide, a drug commonly prescribed for insomnia and nervous tension, was capable of producing malformations in a fetus. The hazard was unmasked when physicians in West Germany and Australia noted a sudden, startling increase in "seal limbs," infant malformations encountered only rarely before (Mintz 1967). There is also the much discussed diethylstilbesterol (DES), a synthetic estrogen that has been used as a "morning after" contraceptive pill. Vaginal and cervical cancer have appeared in over 100 teenage daughters whose mothers took DES during pregnancy, thinking—as did obstetricians— that it would prevent miscarriage (Herbst et al. 1971). A more recent study shows that male children are also affected (Bibbo et al. 1977). Recent investigations have aroused suspicions about the teratogenic potential of widely prescribed tranquilizers, such as Equanil, Miltown, and Librium, when taken during the first six weeks of pregnancy (Milkovich and van den Berg 1974; Saxen 1975; Safra and Oakley 1975). To document the teratogenic time bomb further we need only look at the abnormal incidence of throat cancer in adults who received X rays as children during the 1930s.

We can learn by listening to children. Over half of the 175 letters written by children to consumer advocate Ralph Nader expressed worry about the state of the environment (Dundes n.d.). Another group of children was concerned about the content of food. Others were worried about the epidemic proportions of drug use and called attention to the ways in which society unwittingly encourages abuse. The message from less articulate children appears in another medium: accidents, homicides, and suicide now account for two-thirds of all fatalities among children over 11 years of age. Over half of the serious crimes in this country are committed by children under 17, many of them attacks against the older generation.

In sum, government and business have created an environment in which children are considerably independent of their families and dependent on government and other large-scale institutions. As non-productive citizens, children are not consulted about how things should be. Women supposedly know more about child rearing than men, but government policies are made principally by males. Many of these policies have operated on the basis of myth more than reality. Households of a single parent and one or more children, previously characteristic of lower-income families, are increasingly common, but the government blithely ignores their concomitant child-care needs. Our hiring practices still assume that a man supports a wife and children, that women who divorce and are awarded child support actually receive it.

Corporations feed our children, clothe our children, and help determine their genetic legacy. The important link is between the child and General Foods, Gerber, and Beech-Nut, as well as the Food and Drug Administration. These are but facets of the hidden hierarchies. What is the role of anthropology?

The Vertical Slice

In 1972 I published a paper entitled "Up the Anthropologist— Perspectives Gained from Studying Up." In that essay I discussed anthropological research in a stratified, complex society. My concern was the mind-set whereby social scientists tend to study down, analyzing the poor, the ethnics, the downtrodden. I was particularly struck at the time by a study of a Washington, D.C., ghetto (Hannerz 1969) which viewed underemployment, heavy drinking, and chronic illegal behavior as characteristics of the ghetto. Surely, I thought, if the author had taken a vertical slice he would have had to conclude that, while such features may have described his ghetto community, they also described much other behavior throughout Washington.

At about the same time, I read a paper by J. Boissevain (1968) that pointed to another mind-set: the focus on groups. Since the 1960s there has been a developing literature on nongroups, on networks, but only very slowly has the challenge to take a vertical slice (e.g., to apply the network model vertically rather than horizontally) been applied to anthropological subject matter. There are some examples, however, in reference to children.

The rubella epidemic of 1963–64 added almost 20,000 deaf children to the U.S. population. These children, dispersed across the country, are isolated from one another except when they are brought together by institutions our society has designated as the managers of the deaf. Using the life history technique, Thomas and James Spradley (1978) published a book, *Deaf Like Me,* about the social meaning of being born deaf in America. The Spradleys analyzed the organization of hierarchies that families dealt with in coping with their children's problems: the medical specialists themselves, the knowledge systems and how they are organized and diffused, the teaching and research hierarchies.

Deaf Like Me illustrates the consequences of relying on institutions whose major goal is their own survival. The notion of responsibility in these institutions is primarily related to organizational goals, and the linkage between parents and institutions reflects the parents' lack of power. In Galanter's terms (1974), the parents are not repeat-players. Because they were novices, the parents in the Spradleys' study initially trusted the experts. But a physician assured a young couple that all would be well when it would not, and later that all was well when it was not. Deafness experts convinced parents that they should not communicate with their deaf children through gestures, and their advice led to years of absent communication. However, as horizontal ties among members of the deaf community increased, parents were able to circumvent the predominant theories of how the deaf learn. Although years of experience were not enough to free parents and their children from "helping professions" that did not help, the horizontal links with other parents altered the dominance of the deafness specialists.

In the Berkeley Complaint Project, which sought to understand how Americans complain about products and services, we investigated a complaint about one child and one law (Gerzon n.d.). An eight-year-old child with his shirttail hanging out was engulfed in flames within two to three seconds after a match touched the cloth. The surgeon who treated the child's severe burns was disturbed. He could not believe that clothing so flammable that it sticks plastic-like to the skin and causes third-degree burns could legally be marketed in America. He suggested that the victim's parents complain to the Consumer Product Safety Commission. Their letter to the commission asked simply: "Why did the shirt burn so rapidly?" One month later the CPSC replied: "Your information has been turned over to appropriate members of our staff who will evaluate it and, if necessary, obtain an official sample of the product for analysis. We will take whatever action is indicated." The parents' question remained unanswered.

In our subsequent field research we examined the roles of the federal flammability laws, W. T. Grant (the retailer), the National Retail Merchants Association, the American Textile Manufacturers Institute, the Senate Commerce Committee, the Cone Mills Corporation, the Department of Commerce, the White House, a presidential campaign finance chairman, the Consumer Product Safety Commission, the Federal Trade Commission, and other hierarchies organizationally related to the child that suffered the burns. This research uncovered an incredible amount of interaction between industry and government groups, with each organization intent on organizational survival. The relationship between these organizations and the family and child affected by their actions was minimal. It was only because the family had persisted and written a letter that they were finally contacted by a Consumer Product Safety Commission field investigator who tried to explain why nonflammable childrens' shirts were unavailable. The investigator described the technical problems associated with polyesters, which become "hard" to the touch when treated with flame-retardant chemicals and lose the soft texture that (according to the CPSC official) consumers want.

Interestingly, the lack of vertical interaction between the family and the government agencies returned the parents to the store where the product was purchased. They filled out insurance forms, and once more delay followed. If the parents persisted in their suit (and we do not know how this case has ended), the manufacturer probably settled out of court. As the general counsel for the manufacturer said, "The jury will invariably go with the child; big business doesn't have much of a chance against children in court."

The parents' question, "Why did the shirt burn so rapidly?" was one that the CPSC was not willing to face. The full answer is as complex as America itself. In tracing a case such as this one, the anthropologist becomes aware of the constraints that organizations place on the people working within them, and of the importance that direct interaction has in influencing decisions. Most large organizations are not set up to be responsive to the public or, in this case, a child.

Some organizations have one-way communications with the child: for instance, the testing companies that have so influenced the content and format of schooling, defining the proper direction of cognitive development. One could say that these companies have a direct tie to the children, but in good part neither parents nor children are aware of these seemingly distant and hidden hierarchies. Think about this observation:

A private and unregulated testing service such as the Princeton Testing Service has the power to decide who becomes a doctor, lawyer, anthropologist, biologist, or nearly anything else in this country. It is, indeed, a gatekeeper. The relationship between the Princeton Testing Service and its young clients is worth studying, particularly for anthropologists. Are there cultural biases implicit in the testing procedures? What happens when the best and the brightest as defined by the Princeton Testing Service enter our law schools and medical schools? Do our medical and legal systems improve? What would be the consequences of other selection procedures?

Sometimes the links between hierarchies and children become more direct by virtue of the law, as in *Freitas et al. vs. Baker/Beech-Nut Corp.*, a case begun when some 760,000 women received personalized letters from Beech-Nut warning them of the risks of homemade baby foods. This letter came hard on the heels of a Consumers Union report that homemade baby foods are, on the whole, more nutritious and wholesome than commercial foods (*Consumer Reports,* August 1975). The legal doctrine of "persons *in loco parentis*" becomes important here. The doctrine, recognizing the special responsibilities required by children's incapacities, places affirmative duties on people who find themselves performing the rearing function. In the nineteenth century, the period when other institutions were beginning to compete with the family in the rearing of children, *in loco parentis* was transformed so as to remove the burden of affirmative duties from the parents and at the same time protect those who acted in lieu of parents from being scrutinized by the state. In school cases of the 1960s, however, the courts decided that the nineteenth-century understanding of *in loco parentis* must be overthrown. Cases such as *Freitas et al. vs. Baker/Beech-Nut Corp.* raise the question of whether *in loco parentis* applies to corporations. Good ethnographic research will contribute to this discussion. After all, feeding a child is still feeding a child.

Conclusion

As modern society has differentiated, as specialized institutions have formed, the technologies that have developed have had a profound effect on American society and, more specifically, on American families and their children. One could say that Americans have been positive in their acceptance of new technology; but we have only just begun to look at what the impact has been. As intermediaries parents have begun to feel they have little or no control over the effects of technology on their children. In the absence of research there are disagreements: some people praise all technology, others castigate it. Both positions are wrong.

Ethnographic research can contribute both to theories of technological effects and to practical changes. Until now, technological impact has often been better reported in the press than in social science literature. Headlines asserting that food companies steadily eliminate breast-feeding; that asbestos and lead in the dust of the city damage children's health; that decaying housing in ghetto areas increases the chance of poor children ingesting lead; that drugs such as Valium have effects on pregnant women; that household pest-control gimmicks emit nerve gas; that children in New Mexico drink radioactive water; that food companies promote foods which cause hypertension, diabetes, nutritional deprivation, cancer, and caries—all these should be but starting points for the anthropologist.

Taboo subjects, an anthropologist might say, are those closest to the sources of power. If matters like those just mentioned have been taboo in social science, it is not a new phenomenon. Bright people used to insist, for example, that America was classless. Much of what now preoccupies social scientists would once have been thought unworthy of serious attention.

The vertical slice, the ethnography of the relations between hierarchies and children, can increase our understanding of power and powerlessness, of distancing mechanisms, and of the evolution of responsibility among all the people involved in feeding, clothing, and sheltering our children.

References

Aries, Philippe
    1962   *Centuries of Childhood.* New York: Vintage.
Bendix, Reinhard
    1964   *Nation-Building and Citizenship.* New York: Wiley.
Bibbo, M., W. B. Gill, F. Azzizi, R. Blough, and V. S. Fang
    1977   Follow-up Study of Male and Female Offspring of DES Exposed Mothers. *Obstetrics and Gynecology* 9: 1–8.
Blum, Arlene, and Bruce Ames
    1977   Flame-Retardant Additives as Possible Cancer Hazards. *Science* 195: 17–23.
Boissevain, Jeremy
    1968   The Place of the Non-Group in the Social Sciences. *Man* 3(4): 542–56.
Boli-Bennett, John, and John W. Meyer
    1978   The Ideology of Childhood and the State: Rules Distinguishing Children in National Constitutions, 1870–1970. *American Sociological Review* 43: 797–812.
DeMause, Floyd
    1974   *The History of Childhood.* New York: Psycohistory Press.

Dundes, Alison
   n.d.   An Analysis of Children's Complaint Letters Written to Ralph Nader. Unpublished ms.

Eisenstadt, S. N.
   1956   *From Generation to Generation.* Glencoe, Ill: Free Press.

Galanter, Marc
   1974   Why the "Haves" Come Out Ahead: Speculations on the Limits of Legal Change. *Law and Society Review* 9(1): 95–160.

Gerzon, Mark
   n.d.   One Child and One Law: Kevin Miller and Federal Flammability Laws. Unpublished manuscript. Berkeley, California.

Hannerz, Ulf
   1969   *Soulside: Inquiries into Ghetto Culture and Community.* New York: Columbia University Press.

Harbison, Frederick, and Charles Myers
   1963   *Educational Manpower and Economic Growth.* New York: McGraw-Hill.

Herbst, A. L., H. Ulfelder, and D. C. Poskanzer
   1971   Adenocarcinoma of the Vagina: Association of Maternal Stilbestrol Therapy with Tumor Appearance in Young Women. *New England Journal of Medicine* 284: 878–81.

Hricko, Andrea, and Melanie Brunt
   1977   *Working for Your Life: A Woman's Guide to Job Health Hazards.* University of California, Berkeley: Labor Occupational Health Program.

Kanter, Rosabeth
   1977   *Work and Family in the United States: A Critical Review and Agenda for Research and Policy.* New York: Russell Sage Foundation.

Katz, Michael
   1968   *The Irony of Early School Reform.* Boston: Beacon Press.

Lasch, Christopher
   1977   *Haven in a Heartless World: The Family Besieged.* New York: Basic Books.

Milkovich, L., and B. J. van den Berg
   1974   Effects of Prenatal Meprobamate and Chlordiazepoxide Hydrochloride on Human Embryonic and Fetal Development. *New England Journal of Medicine* 291: 1268–71.

Mintz, Morton
   1967   *By Prescription Only.* Boston: Beacon Press.

Nader, Laura
   1972   Up the Anthropologist—Perspectives Gained from Studying Up. In D. Hymes (ed.), *Reinventing Anthropology.* New York: Random House.
   1978   Hit and Run—Multinationals on a Collision Course with Humanity. In *Responsibilities of Multinational Corporations to Societies*, vol. 1. Washington, D.C.: Council of Better Business Bureaus.

Safra, M. J., and J. P. Oakley
   1975   Association Between Cleft Lip With or Without Cleft Palate and Prenatal Exposure to Diazepam. *Lancet* 2: 478–540.

Saxen, I.
   1975   Association Between Oral Clefts and Drugs Taken During Preg-

nancy. *International Journal of Epidemiology and Community Health* 4: 37–44.

Schroeder, Henry D.
1974   *The Poisons Around Us: Toxic Metals in Food, Air and Water.* Bloomington: Indiana University Press.

Spradley, Thomas S., and James P. Spradley
1978   *Deaf Like Me.* New York: Random House.

Whiting, Beatrice
1963   *Six Cultures: Studies of Child Rearing.* New York: Wiley.

Zaretsky, Eli
1976   *Capitalism: The Family and Personal Life.* New York: Harper and Row.

Zimmerman, C., and M. Frampton
1935   *Family and Society: A Study of the Sociology of Reconstruction.* London: Williams and Norgate, Ltd.

4.

The Bureaucratic Context
of a Community Mental Health Center:
The View from "Up"

HELEN B. SCHWARTZMAN

Anthropologists have traditionally studied small-scale, nonindustrialized, "primitive" societies. Many such societies have come to be influenced by industrialization and urbanization, and anthropologists have therefore focused attention on the study of these processes. In coming to terms with the effects of modernization on "primitive" cultures, however, ethnographers have been reluctant to modernize their own discipline. Even as they have begun to "bring it all back home," anthropologists have pursued the primitive, both literally and metaphorically, into the urban context by continuing to identify their subject matter as the study of the exotic, the peculiar, and particularly, as Nader (1972: 289) has suggested, the powerless.

We continue to base many of our anthropological investigations on the idea that the cultural, subcultural, ethnic, and organizational groups we study exist in isolation from larger political and economic units. Even in cases where the influence of these contexts is taken into account and recommendations are formulated about what to do about specific problems, we continue to complain that bureaucrats pay no attention to our research, never follow our recommendations, and do not even seem to know that anthropologists exist. All this, however, should only encourage us to study their culture in order to understand what they do listen to, how they understand it, and why. In this paper the bureaucratic context of a community mental health center (CMHC) is examined in order to (1) suggest a way of interpreting the problematic history of many such organizations, and (2) to urge anthropologists to consider the effect of the bureaucratic context on populations and problems that we have traditionally studied.

The Paper Context

In the field of medical anthropology four types of studies tend to be made: (1) investigations of cultural components in the etiology and incidence of illness (e.g., Scotch and Geiger 1962); (2) studies of popular reactions to programs of health maintenance and health improvement (e.g., Paul and Miller 1955); (3) research on the organizational culture of particular treatment facilities such as mental hospitals (e.g., Caudill 1958); and (4) studies of health care and healing behavior in various cultural and subcultural settings (e.g., Gonzalez 1964). All these studies are important; however, the researchers frequently neglect one very significant context—the effect of federal, state, city, university, or private-agency bureaucratic structures on the communities, programs, and institutions studied.[1]

This neglect is clearly illustrated in studies of community mental health centers. Such centers are affected by three major contexts: (1) *the community or neighborhood context,* which may be both a geographic and a social reality, encompassing various communities and groups which define themselves as existing together in a specific area; (2) *the organizational context,* which is created by interactions of staff members with one another, with patients, with board members, with community residents, and so on;[2] and finally, (3) *the bureaucratic context,* which is defined as the relationship existing between a center and its major funding sources, generally some combination of federal, state, and local mental health agencies. This last context is perhaps most appropriately referred to as "the paper context" because it is visible for the most part only on paper—in forms, regulations, policy statements, legislation, and, most importantly, pay checks. The paper context is the least tangible of these contexts—as it is generally the least visible in the form of personnel—but it is often also the most consequential, because its regulations and policies often dictate or constrain the actions of a center and its staff.

There are relatively few studies of CMHCs by anthropologists, and these generally concern a center's existence within, and relevance to, its community or neighborhood context (e.g., Schensul 1972; Sevilla-Casas 1972). It has been left to investigators from other disciplines to analyze CMHCs' relationship to federal, state, and local bureaucracies (e.g., Connery 1968; Mechanic 1969; B. and J. Ehrenreich 1970; Chu and Trotter 1974).

Midwest Community Mental Health Center

Between January 1975 and July 1976, I took part in a team research study of a community mental health center located in a low-income, multi-ethnic community of a large midwestern city. This study was designed to investigate the historical development of what will be called here Midwest Community Mental Health Center, particularly the influence of the three above-mentioned major contexts of a center's activities.[3]

The Community Mental Health Centers Act, passed by Congress in 1963 (P.L. 88–164), marked the initiation of the CMHC movement in this country. At the time it was thought to be an innovative, even revolutionary, approach to the treatment of mental illness. Looking back at the initial enthusiasm generated by this movement, an anthropologist might well classify it as charismatic or millenarian. As Chu and Trotter suggest in the Ralph Nader Study Group report on CMHCs and the National Institute of Mental Health (NIMH), it was thought "that the CMHC would usher in the millennium for mental health services" (1974: 3). All CMHCs were required by NIMH regulations to provide five kinds of essential services: (1) inpatient services, (2) outpatient services, (3) partial hospitalization, (4) 24-hour emergency services, and (5) consultation and education services. All centers were also required to serve a geographically designated "catchment area" with a population of no fewer than 75,000 and no more than 200,000.

In the early 1970s Midwest CMHC was funded by an NIMH staffing grant as a free-standing, comprehensive CMHC. According to the grant proposal, a community board was to be responsible for center operations and for the hiring of a director. The grant stressed community participation through board membership, the use of paraprofessional staff drawn from the community, and a consortium model of service delivery to a specifically designated catchment area. This particular catchment area contained a large number of "at-risk" populations, the most obvious being numerous ex-mental patients who had been "dumped" or "deinstitutionalized" (depending on whom you talked to) into the community during the 1960s.

Midwest CMHC began enthusiastically, with much talk of its being a new solution to the mental and social problems of the area, and with a feeling that this was *the* community's mental health center. However, the center quickly encountered, and seemed to engender, criticism both from within and from without (from affiliated and nonaffiliated agencies, from board members, staff, etc.). It was felt, for example, that staff were not "out in the community" enough; they weren't "doing treatment"; too much time was spent in training; too little time was spent in training; staff wanted to solve too many different types of problems; the center was not establishing effective programs; the programs were not meeting "community needs"; the paraprofessionals were given too much power and the professionals too little; the paraprofessionals were given too little power and the professionals too much; staff (particularly certain staff) were incompetent; board members (particularly certain board members) were incompetent; the State Mental Health Department would not cooperate with the center; the State Mental Health Department interfered too much in center activities and made inappropriate demands for records, statistics, etc.; the center was too crisis oriented and never engaged in appropriate long-range planning; the state of the center's finances was constantly a problem, and so on.

After the first two years, center programs were established and a variety of services were being offered. However, hostile and suspicious cliques and factions had by now been formed and there was a tendency to personalize issues and scapegoat individuals as the cause of all the problems. Center personnel in many respects turned inward, forever examining and criticizing their own actions and reactions. (What is the real role of the board? What is the relation of the director to the board, to the staff, to the community at large? Are not staff also community members? etc., etc.) This constant self-criticism did not totally deter the delivery of mental health services but it did cause serious problems for all concerned. There was a high staff turnover,[4] a constant crisis orientation, and a feeling of hostility and suspiciousness surrounding all group and individual interactions (staff were hostile to board members, board members were hostile to staff, other agency personnel were hostile to both staff and board members, and so on). There was likewise a great concern with personal pathology and a considerable amount of namecalling—"he's crazy," "she's paranoid," "they're really sick"—as well as actual hospitalization of some staff. One of the most frequent comments about the center heard from all participants was that "this is a crazy, out-of-control place," or "it's incredible how the center does terrible things to the people that work here," or "the people are nice but the place is crazy."

This brief description glosses over much that happened in the center's early years of existence, and it does not depict the current situation at the center. However, even though the events may sound strange, they have their parallel in studies of other CMHCs (e.g., Panzetta 1971; Shaw and Eagle 1971; Sloan 1972; Kaplan and Roman 1973) as well as other social service organizations (e.g., see Freudenberger's 1974 discussion of staff "burn-out" in the free clinic movement; Molica and Winn's 1974 description of the problem of "infighting" in a free drug clinic; and Hern, Gold, and Oakes' 1977 discussion of authority conflicts and confusion in abortion clinics).

There are several explanations why CMHCs should have such problematic, conflictual histories: (1) This is to be expected in the natural evolution of such organizations; "it's a phase." (2) The center reflects and mirrors the community/catchment area in which it exists. If the community is disorganized, then the center will reflect the disorganization and pathology of its community. (3) The problems stem from the use of the paraprofessional model, and/or are the result of particularly problematic or "troublemaker" staff or board members who act out their personal "craziness" in the organizational context. (4) The problems are "built into" the centers in their grants and in the guidelines used to set up such programs.

Each of these explanations has some merit to it and clearly no one is likely to explain the entire phenomenon. It can be seen, however, that each interpretation places responsibility for center problems on one or another of the above-mentioned contexts, i.e., (1) the community; (2) the organization,[5] or particular individuals within it; or (3) bureaucratic guidelines and regulations. Though recognizing that each context influences the operation and delivery of center services in very important ways, I will consider in the remainder of this chapter only the effect of the bureaucratic context on a center's problematic operations.

The CMHC: Old Metaphors for New Programs

It is my suggestion that the legislation, policies, and guidelines used by federal and state bureaucracies for "dealing with" CMHCs were based on models utilized for the creation and operation of total institutions, such as mental hospitals, and not on models appropriate for the operation of community-based service delivery systems. This is not, however, the same argument advanced by Chu and Trotter (1974), who maintained that the problem with the CMHC program is that the prevalence and dominance of the medical model and of medical personnel encouraged the creation of CMHCs as "mini-hospitals" in the image of mental hospitals. Rather, it is argued here that a total institution model was imposed on the conceptualization of the CMHC system with somewhat different consequences. In this system the model appears in conceptualizations of the *community as a mental hospital*— and for Midwest CMHC this was more than an analogy, given the presence of large numbers of ex-mental patients residing in the community, and given the fact that community residents often referred to the area as a "psychiatric ghetto." It is also my suggestion that CMHCs are related to as if *they are patients* "in the hospital." This may sound peculiar, but it is really the logical consequence of a state mental health department, encouraged by federal financial support, attempting to move out of the business of direct service, but continuing to use an institutional model of direct service to patients for establishing relations with new direct service providers (i.e., community mental health agencies). The funding bureaucracies have placed a community agency between themselves and individual patients without changing the model of the relationship, placing these new agencies in the role of the patient *in* the hospital (i.e., community).

How does this transformation happen, and how does it manifest itself both in conceptualization and in actual practice? In order to clarify the argument, some of the major characteristics of mental hospitals, the relationships that they create and maintain between staff and patients, and the behavior that they both create and expect in patients must briefly be reviewed. Though many researchers have discussed these issues, Goffman's discussion of characteristics of mental hospitals as total institutions, in his classic study *Asylums* (1961), will be used here. Several of these characteristics are briefly described below, followed by suggested analogies in the CMHC system.

1. *Confinement.* Total institutions are said by Goffman to be encompassing "to the extent that barriers to social intercourse with the outside and to departure . . . [are] often built right into the physical plant, such as locked doors, high walls, barbed wire . . . " (1961: 4).

Catchment Area Concept. In the CMHC model the idea of confinement appears most obviously in the catchment area concept. Catchment areas serve to confine, contain, and encompass CMHCs, defining the nature of community by geography, rather than by ethnic, neighborhood, block, religious, political, or other affiliation. Though this definition stresses geographic responsibility, it often creates arbitrary and unnecessary barriers to service, as well as conflicts with other geographic divisions—e.g., political jurisdictions, school districts, police districts, and so on. The fact that there can be only one CMHC in every catchment area reduces competition, often encouraging poor quality of service. In some instances, however, a state may fund a CMHC, another provider agency, and even its own outpatient service in the same area, which increases competition for funds without a corresponding competition in the quality of service. Unfortunately, this funding competition occurs in a system which is supposed to emphasize and encourage coordination of services. Also tied to the catchment area concept are restrictions on the type of grant which may be awarded (e.g., grants to designated poverty areas decline less than those to nonpoverty areas) and, therefore, on the type of funding to be secured by the center.[6]

2. *Surveillance.*   According to Goffman another feature of mental hospitals as total institutions is the necessity for surveillance.

> In total institutions where persons are moved in blocks they can be most efficiently supervised by personnel whose chief activity . . . is surveillance . . . a seeing to it that everyone does what he has been clearly told is required of him, under conditions where one person's infraction is likely to stand out in relief against the visible, constantly examined compliance of the others. . . . A basic split develops between a large managed group, "inmates," and a small supervisory staff. Each group tends to conceive of the other in terms of narrow, hostile stereotypes: staff see inmates as bitter, secretive and untrustworthy, while inmates see staff as condescending, high-handed and mean. [1961: 7]

According to Goffman, surveillance staff also control communication from inmates to higher staff levels (p. 8) and vice versa; the inmate is generally excluded from (or mystified by) the decisions taken by staff regarding his fate (p. 9).

Monitoring.   In order to insure that CMHCs are doing what they have been funded to do, state and federal authorities set standards and create guidelines for the funding and operation of such programs. It is therefore necessary for these bureaucracies to monitor the centers to make sure they are doing what they have been told—to see if they are in compliance with legislation, regulations, and guidelines. Catchment area monitors and/or state generalists in HEW regional offices are responsible for surveying centers in this fashion. These monitors often control the upward flow of information from centers to higher-level state or federal personnel and, likewise, they often control and interpret information and new regulations flowing downward. From the perspective of center personnel, gaining knowledge about how decisions are made about their future funding status (e.g., what statistics are used, what services are seen as appropriate or inappropriate) is often a very confusing and mystifying, if not an altogether impossible, process. Center monitors often come to be seen in the stereotyped images of gods or demons, and this leads to a great deal of misinterpretation of information by all parties concerned—and a constant need for reinterpretation.

3. *Dependency.*   Patients in mental hospitals are totally dependent on staff and on the hospital itself for all their basic needs (e.g., food, shelter, clothing, etc.). According to Goffman, patients are even obligated "to request permission or supplies for minor activities that one can execute on one's own on the outside, such as smoking, shaving,

going to the toilet. . . . This obligation not only puts the individuals in a submissive or suppliant role 'unnatural' for an adult but also opens up his line of action to interceptions by staff" (1961: 41).

Granting. The granting of money, in the form of federal construction or staffing grants and federal and/or state grants-in-aid, similarly fosters varying degrees of dependency in the CMHC system. For example, federal staffing grants to free-standing centers may be said to encourage two kinds of dependency. In the first instance, a center may become depéndent on NIMH for continuing support, particularly since there are few built-in requirements for centers to achieve any degree of financial self-sufficiency (e.g., little encouragement to collect fees even when appropriate), and since the expectation of support from the private sector has now unanimously been declared unrealistic.[7] Monies expected from in-patient payments are also an unrealizable dream, given hospital arrangements and structures. And in fact this arrangement is contradictory to CMHC goals, since a center designed to treat people in the community should not be expected to generate a large portion of its operating funds by keeping people in local hospitals. A second type of dependency is created by declining grant arrangements and staffing grant constraints imposed by NIMH, which make it necessary for a center to depend for funds for space, equipment, etc., on state resources; as the amount of the NIMH grant declines yearly, the center becomes increasingly dependent on the state.

4. *Conflicting and Contradictory Standards and Demands.* Goffman suggests that "the standards of treatment that one inmate has a right to expect may often conflict . . . with the standards desired by another . . . " (1961: 78). For example, if the grounds gate of an institution is to be left open for patients on "town parole," it may be that some patients who could otherwise be allowed on the grounds will have to be kept on a locked ward. According to Goffman, in total institutions there is also "a constant conflict between humane standards on one hand and institutional efficiency on the other" (1961: 78). At another level, Bateson's (1956) double-bind theory of schizophrenia, as well as the findings of Stanton and Schwartz's study of institutional participation in psychiatric illness and treatment, as reported in their book *The Mental Hospital* (1954), appear to indicate that contradictory or paradoxical demands, standards, or directives are at least contributory to the genesis and/or the encouragement and perpetuation of symptomatic behavior in patients.

Service Priorities. Conflicting demands are particularly evident in the CMHC system in the area of service priorities, since a center may be placed in the confusing position of having to deal with contradictory state and federal policies in regard to types of services provided. Midwest CMHC was placed in such an awkward position. To secure state funds, Midwest had to focus on the treatment of priority patients, defined by the state as former state hospital patients. At the same time, federal agencies mandated a focus on consultation and education programs, or primary prevention, which the state refused to support, not allowing its money to be used as a matching source to secure federal funds. This led to the use of a number of statistical and funding deception devices in order to live up to (or at least appear to live up to) conflicting federal and state demands, and a "damned if you do, damned if you don't" attitude on the part of staff.

5. *Looping.*   Goffman reports that a "looping" process is characteristic of many mental health facilities.

> In many psychiatric establishments a permissive atmosphere is felt to encourage the inmate to "project" or "act out" his typical difficulties in living, which can then be brought to his attention during group therapy sessions. . . . Through the process of looping, . . . the inmate's reaction to his own situation is collapsed back into this situation itself, and he is not allowed to retain the usual segregation of these phases of action. [1961: 37]

The CMHC Form of Looping.   A similar process occurs in a number of areas in the CMHC system, particularly in the financial area. Here, as has already been suggested, a permissive and/or unpredictable atmosphere has been created in which centers often "act out" financially by chalking up deficits and/or other financial problems which may then be "written off" by federal or state administrators (and rationalized as "part of the growing pains process"), but then "looped" back onto the center's general reputation as an incompetent, problematic place. Likewise, the financial, statistical, and record-keeping deceptions encouraged by conflicting state and federal demands may be looped back onto the center's reputation for running a deceptive, secretive, and untrustworthy program.

6. *Self-Concern.*   Finally, a sixth characteristic discussed by Goffman relates to a particular type of self-concern exhibited by the inmate in the total institution.

> In many total institutions a peculiar kind of level of self-concern is engendered. The low position of inmates . . . creates a milieu of personal failure in which one's fall from grace is continuously pressed home. In response, the inmate tends to develop a story, or line, a sad tale—a kind of lamentation and apologia—which he constantly tells to his fellows as a

means of accounting for his present low estate. In consequence, the inmate's self may become even more a focus of his conversation and concern than it does on the outside, leading to much self-pity. [1961: 67]

Inward Focus.   The analogy between CMHCs' and inmates' self-concern and self-pity is certainly suggested by the events described above that occurred during the early years of Midwest CMHC's operations. As also mentioned above, the inward focus of center personnel has been documented in a number of other studies of CMHCs, e.g., Panzetta (1971) and Kaplan and Roman (1973). This inward focus, a concentration on self-examination and self-critique, with the subsequent development of both individual and center-wide stories, laments, and jokes about the center's problems, appears to match the excessive self-concern, self-pity, and self-mocking behavior said to be characteristic of inmates (and specifically patients as inmates). One particularly interesting story/analogy, collected in an interview with a staff member, portrays Midwest CMHC as a "Wild West boom town." The participation of the center's funding bureaucracies in the creation of this "boom town" and the consequences for the center are evident in this amusing description.

> I've described Midwest as being a boom town and about 1850 the wild, wild West and what happened is that Uncle Sam and Washington said, "Hey man, there's gold in them thar hills," and everybody rushed right over to get the gold and the organizers came along. The state [mental health department] and the feds came along with it and said, "Well, you have this boom town, but you really need somebody to build the houses and things like that." So they built these shacks and shanties and they got somebody from Washington to be the mayor of the town, to run it and everybody was happy ever after. And it was really gaudy too, they had all kinds of saloons and houses of ill-repute and everybody had the God-damndest good time you've ever seen. But what they forgot to do, of course, was to build sewage systems and provide adequate law enforcement to keep certain things, banks, solvent and all the other things that a place needs; they just neglected, forgot it totally which meant one day no fire department, one day one of the shacks goes up and then the whole town. Also the gold is running out and they're frantically running around looking for other sources of gold "in them thar hills" and it's becoming unreal. . . .

Conclusion

In 1963 John F. Kennedy's message to the Congress concerning mental illness and retardation contained what were at the time very stirring words:[8]

Services to the mentally ill and to the mentally retarded must be community-based and provide a range of services to meet community needs. It is with these objectives in mind that I am proposing a new approach to mental illness and mental retardation. This approach is designed, in large measure, to use Federal reserves to stimulate state, local, and private action. When carried out, reliance on the cold mercy of custodial isolation will be supplanted by the open warmth of community concern and capability. Emphasis on prevention, treatment and rehabilitation will be substituted for a desultory interest in confining patients in an institution to wither away. [1963: 3]

As has been argued by others (e.g., Chu and Trotter 1974), and as is argued in this paper, the "bold, new approach" of the community mental health program was in many ways a reformulation of the "traditional, old approach." It has been suggested here that the conceptualization of the CMHC system was influenced by traditional approaches utilized for the management of persons in total institutions, particularly mental hospitals. In this instance the only changes to occur were the creation of a new context for the hospital and the placement of organizations, not individuals, in the patient role.[9]

It may be that many other types of social service organizations, as well as the populations that they serve, experience a similar application of this total institution model by federal, state, and/or local funding bureaucracies. A possible example, one that is probably most familiar to anthropologists, is the experience of Native Americans on reservations, and of Native American organizations in both rural and urban areas. The use of this model for structuring relationships with problematic (and often powerless) groups is particularly effective when it transforms these groups into patients or patient-like entities; such designations can then serve to explain these groups' problems (as well as to create and/or perpetuate the existence of symptomatic behavior among individual members; see Goffman's 1961 discussion of "looping" described above, and also J. Schwartzman and P. Bokos 1979). This model should be a useful concept for examining the bureaucratic context of other social service organizations and the populations they serve.[10]

In discussing the approach anthropologists should take in the study of health problems, and particularly mental health problems, Maretzki suggests the following:

We propose that the entire handling of health related problems needs to be revolutionized in our society and in all those which have borrowed our model. Nothing short of a complete overhaul of the present established way of responding is likely to make much difference. Anthropologists have pleaded with the NIMH to gain permission for studies of decision making in that institution which for years has set the patterns for national mental health programs. Without such a study, how can we expect others in the country to accept us in the role we see for ourselves? We would like to do the same in hospitals, in clinics, in community mental health centers, and even in the sanctums of private practitioners who need interpret our request no differently than the many respondents throughout the world who have contributed so much to our anthropological knowledge of other cultures. [1973: 137]

If anthropologists want to study the bureaucratization of health, and particularly mental health, in the United States they must now stop wishing and pleading and start acting. This study of one CMHC took the researchers not only into the system of formal and informal social relationships of the program, but also into the streets and neighborhoods of the center's community, and finally into the corridors of state and federal office buildings and the paper maze of regulations, guidelines, legislation, and policies. From the brief analysis attempted here, it can be seen that the paper context greatly affects the communities in which mental health programs exist, as well as the organizational community of the center itself. I suggest that this context is amenable to ethnographic research methods if only we decide that it is appropriate (and, in fact, crucial) for anthropologists to investigate. In this sense it is possible to argue that just as the CMHC system has been limited and constrained by traditional models of mental hospital management, so too are anthropologists limited and constrained by our traditional models of appropriate research topics and populations.

Acknowledgments

The research on which this paper is based was performed by a team that included, in addition to the author, Anita Kneifel, Don Merten, and Gary Schwartz, whom I would like to thank for their collaboration on the project and their comments on this paper. I would also like to thank John Schwartzman, Merton S. Krause, and Anne Seiden for their suggestions and criticism. I am also very grateful to all of the individuals involved with Midwest Community Mental Health Center for their participation and interest in this study. Finally, I would like to thank Estelle Marvel for her assistance in preparing this paper for publication.

Notes

1. Recently, however, some anthropologists have begun to recognize the importance of studying this context (e.g., Pelto 1975). Also, at the 1976

American Anthropological Association Annual Meeting in Washington, D.C., James Spradley organized a medical anthropology roundtable luncheon discussion entitled "Up the Health Care System: Strategies for Studying the Policy Makers."

2. Of course, these interactions are formally affected by the hierarchical and bureaucratic structure of the center itself.

3. For the purposes of this project, research material was obtained from a number of different sources: participant observation; formal and informal interviews with various participants in the center's early initiation and formulation and its current operation; and analysis of documents (e.g., grant proposal, legislation, regulations, guidelines, minutes, memos, etc.).

4. When we completed our research in 1976 approximately 55 to 60 percent of the center's staff had "turned over" during the year and a half of our project's duration. As ethnographers we were placed in the unusual position of remaining in the research site longer than many of our informants.

5. For an analysis of problems existing between conflicting groups (or cultures) *within* Midwest CMHC, see Schwartzman, Kneifel, and Krause (1978).

6. See Panzetta's (1971) useful discussion of problems of the catchment area concept and the effect of this idea on CMHCs.

7. See Chu and Trotter (1974) for further discussion of the financial status of CMHCs.

8. It should be noted here that this message was the first of its kind on this subject to be delivered by a president of the United States.

9. This view of the CMHC system was suggested again in a return visit made to Midwest CMHC a few months after the completion of fieldwork. During this visit I noticed that a door (which I was told would soon be locked) had been installed between the lobby or patient waiting room area(which opens directly onto the street) and staff offices and meeting areas. An unusual logic must be at work here, creating as it has a situation where staff confine themselves behind closed and locked doors which serve to keep staff *in* and patients *out*.

10. In this regard, Basham (1976) presents an extremely interesting analysis of "the structural and behavioral parallels common to total institutions and ethnic situations" (p. 15).

References

Basham, R.
    1976   Ethnicity as a Total Institution. In *Proceedings of the Central States Anthropological Society, Selected Papers,* vol. 2. Ann Arbor, Michigan: CSAS.

Bateson, G., D. Jackson, J. Haley, and J. Weakland
    1956   Toward a Theory of Schizophrenia. *Behavioral Science* 1: 251–64.

Caudill, W.
    1958   *The Psychiatric Hospital as a Small Society.* Published for the Commonwealth Fund. Cambridge, Mass.: Harvard University Press.

Chu, F. D., and S. Trotter
  1974   *The Madness Establishment: Ralph Nader's Study Group Report on
           the National Institute of Mental Health.* New York: Grossman.
Connery, R. H., et al.
  1968   *The Politics of Mental Health: Organizing Community Mental
           Health in Metropolitan Areas.* New York: Columbia University
           Press.
Ehrenreich, B., and J. Ehrenreich
  1970   *The American Health Empire: Power, Profits, and Politics.* A
           Report Prepared for the Health Policy Advisory Center (Health-
           PAC). New York: Random House/Vintage.
Freudenberger, H. J.
  1974   Staff Burn-Out. *Journal of Social Issues* 30: 159–65.
Goffman, E.
  1961   *Asylums.* Garden City, N.Y.: Doubleday/Anchor.
Gonzalez, N. L. S.
  1964   Beliefs and Practices Concerning Medicine and Nutrition Among
           Lower Class Urban Guatemalans. *American Journal of Public
           Health* 54: 1726–34.
Hern, W. M., M. R. Gold, and A. Oakes
  1977   Administrative Incongruence and Authority Conflict in Four
           Abortion Clinics. *Human Organization* 36: 376–83.
Kaplan, S. R. and M. Roman
  1973   *The Organization and Delivery of Mental Health Services in the
           Ghetto: The Lincoln Hospital Experience.* New York: Praeger.
Kennedy, J. F.
  1963   Message from the President of the United States Relative to Mental
           Illness and Mental Retardation. 88th Congress, 1st Session, House
           Document no. 48. Washington, D.C.: Government Printing Office.
Maretzki, T. W.
  1973   Epilogue. In L. Nader and T. W. Maretzki (eds.), *Cultural Illness
           and Health: Essays in Human Adaptation.* Anthropological Studies
           no. 9. Washington, D.C.: American Anthropological Association.
Mechanic, D.
  1969   *Mental Health and Social Policy.* Englewood Cliffs, N.J.: Prentice-
           Hall.
Molica, G. J., and N. E. Winn
  1974   History of the Waikiki Clinic. *Journal of Social Issues* 30: 53–60.
Nader, L.
  1972   Up the Anthropologist—Perspectives Gained from Studying Up. In
           D. Hymes (ed.), *Reinventing Anthropology.* New York: Random
           House/Vintage.
Panzetta, A. F.
  1971   *Community Mental Health: Myth and Reality.* Philadelphia: Lea
           and Febiger.
Paul, B., and W. B. Miller (eds.)
  1955   *Health, Culture, and Community: Case Studies of Public Reactions
           to Health Programs.* New York: Russell Sage Foundation.
Pelto, P.
  1975   Medicine, Anthropology, Community: An Overview. Paper pre-
           sented at 74th Annual Meeting of the American Anthropological
           Association, San Francisco, 2-6 December.

Schensul, S.
  1972   Strategies in Relating Research to Community Development. Paper
          presented at 71st Annual Meeting of the American Anthropological
          Association, Toronto, Ontario.
Schwartzman, H. B., A. W. Kneifel, and M. S. Krause
  1978   Culture Conflict in a Community Mental Health Center. *Journal of
          Social Issues* 34: 93–110.
Schwartzman, J., and P. Bokos
  1979   Methadone Maintenance: The Addict's Family Recreated. *The
          International Journal of Family Therapy* 1: 338–55.
Scotch, N., and H. J. Geiger
  1962   The Epidemiology of Rheumatoid Arthritis. *Journal of Chronic
          Diseases* 15: 1037–67.
Sevilla-Casas, E.
  1972   A Model for Anthropological Research in a Psychiatric Setting.
          Paper presented at 71st Annual Meeting of the American Anthropo-
          logical Association, Toronto, Ontario.
Shaw, R., and C. J. Eagle
  1971   Programmed Failure: The Lincoln Hospital Story. *Community
          Mental Health Journal* 7: 355–63.
Sloan, B.
  1972   The Temple University Community Mental Health Center. Paper
          presented at Annual Meeting of Professors West of the Mississippi,
          University of California, San Diego.
Stanton, A. S., and M. S. Schwartz
  1954   *The Mental Hospital.* New York: Basic Books.

5.

Bureaucracy and Innovation:
An American Case

GERALD M. BRITAN AND MICHAEL CHIBNIK

In the past two decades anthropologists have increasingly turned from the study of small societies to the study of modern nation-states. With few exceptions, however, their research has sought out structural equivalents to social and cultural phenomena that had been studied before, concentrating on small and isolated social segments, such as ethnic subcultures, rural hamlets, and urban neighborhoods. Although theorists have analyzed these little "communities" in relation to wider regional, national, and international systems (Wolf and Cole 1974; Britan and Denich 1976), their research usually remains bound to theoretical constructs more appropriate to other times and places.

Bureaucracy is the most pervasive organizational form of complex societies. The governmental and industrial bureaucracies that make most of the important policy decisions affecting people's lives must be examined if the hierarchical structure of modern states is to be understood. Yet while anthropologists realize that their studies must be placed within a broader institutional context, the nature of bureaucracies has rarely been considered (Nader 1972; Foster 1969).

Some recent trends, however, suggest that this lack will soon be remedied. In the past few years anthropologists have become increasingly involved in evaluation research, assessing the results of social action programs. In principle, such assessments of program results require an understanding of how programs operate and a more careful examination of the dynamics of bureaucracies. Still, anthropological researchers have usually been employees of bureaucracies, not their evaluators. They have been hired to analyze program effects, not to assess program operations. As a result, their evaluations have usually taught us little about how bureaucracies work.

For two years, from 1975 through 1977, we conducted a program evaluation that provided an unusually detailed perspective on the workings of federal agencies. This research has provided us with a number of insights about the nature of bureaucracy and has suggested a number of topics for further anthropological study.

The Experimental Technology Incentives Program

The enormous importance of technological change to America's economic growth has only recently been recognized by economists (Hufbauer 1966; Vernon 1966; Keesing 1967). By the late 1960s the federal government became increasingly concerned that the rate of technological innovation in the United States was slowing. As a result two programs were created in 1972 to "determine ways of stimulating nonfederal investment in R&D results" (Nixon 1972). One of these efforts was the Experimental Technology Incentives Program. Its purpose is to examine the relationship between government activities and technological innovation in order to formulate new public policies that can better stimulate technological change. The program's central assumption is that private industry is capable of developing technology "efficiently" if barriers to innovation are removed and appropriate incentives provided. ETIP focuses on a wide range of government actions that indirectly affect innovation by altering the economic environment in which it occurs.

ETIP realizes that to develop effective policy changes it must work closely with relevant federal agencies. However, it is very difficult to convince an agency to make a major policy shift merely on the basis of a hypothesized technological effect. Unsuccessful changes could have serious repercussions, not only on ETIP and the agencies, but also on the nation's economy. ETIP's strategy therefore has been to develop incremental policy "experiments" that provide real-world tests of policy hypotheses and at the same time supply agencies with the experience needed to make wider application possible.

Since its founding, ETIP has developed numerous projects with agencies such as the Federal Supply Service, the Federal Power Commission, the Nuclear Regulatory Agency, the Environmental Protection Agency, the Federal Rail Administration, and the Food and Drug Administration. These projects are concerned with such diverse issues as government purchases of new air conditioners, the development of nuclear reactor standards, the control of critical commodity shortages, and the setting of electric utility rates.

Our Involvement

Although ETIP's purpose is to conduct experiments, in many ways it can be seen as an experiment itself, an attempt to institutionalize a source of policy change within the federal bureaucracy. In 1973, a special ETIP Evaluation Panel composed of prominent economists, scientists, and businessmen was established at the National Academy of Sciences. This panel periodically reviews program activities and formulates recommendations for ETIP's supervisors at the Department of Commerce and the National Bureau of Standards. The panel, however, wanted fuller information than its periodic meetings with ETIP staff could provide. In 1974 it decided that

> unlike experiments in the physical sciences, there are no clear measures of output to test the effect of ETIP-initiated intervention. . . . Sociologists and social anthropologists have developed observational methodologies for assessing the impact of interventions and for analyzing the contributing factors that determine the extent of that impact. The Panel, therefore, recommends that one or more sociologists/social anthropologists make a fieldcase evaluation of ETIP intervention experiments . . . to evaluate ETIP as an experiment . . . [and] the impact of its sponsored programs . . . in participating government agencies. [ETIP Evaluation Panel 1974: 4-5]

The panel hoped to learn more about the extent of agency cooperation ETIP had obtained, the degree to which important technological change issues had been addressed, and the likelihood that improved federal policies could be identified and implemented.

In June of 1975 one of the authors of this paper (Britan) was given a contract by the National Academy of Sciences to carry out such a study. The other author (Chibnik) was hired by Britan to aid in the evaluation.[1]

Research Methods

Since most of ETIP's projects involve complicated technological, economic, and organizational questions, the initial part of our research tried to gain a more accurate picture of the nature of program operations and the scope of program activities. This involved an investigation not only of formal procedures and goals but also of informal understandings and processes. Several months were spent interviewing ETIP staff, examining document files, compiling information on projects, and completing a preliminary analysis of program characteristics.

The most important questions about ETIP, however, involve its

relationships with agencies, and the next phase of research concentrated
on this topic. Intensive case studies of eleven ETIP projects were
conducted to supplement the picture provided by staff interviews and by
documents, and to gain a better understanding of project development.
The case studies supply information about several crucial aspects of
ETIP-agency interaction, including (1) reasons for agency decisions to
participate in ETIP projects, (2) reasons for any ETIP-agency conflicts,
(3) the nature of informal ETIP and agency understandings, and (4) the
nature of the political and organizational climate in which projects
develop. Numerous interviews with ETIP and agency staff, private
contractors, and relevant outsiders were conducted, and reports and
publications bearing on historical and theoretical issues associated with
particular projects were studied.

During the year and a half of evaluation a number of significant
shifts occurred. New projects were developed; existing projects changed;
and ETIP's internal organization, goals, and understandings altered.
Project summaries were periodically updated and follow-up interviews
conducted so that a diachronic perspective could be obtained.

Finally, our qualitative and quantitative data were assessed and a
four-part report was prepared for the National Academy. The first
volume of this report summarizes our findings and recommendations,
the second provides an ethnographic overview of ETIP and its place in
the bureaucracy, the third contains the eleven project case studies, and
the fourth is an appendix of analytical and summary tables. This report
was a major input to a Department of Commerce evaluation of ETIP in
the summer of 1977, which resulted in a major program restructuring.

An Overview of Bureaucratic Process

As our research proceeded, we came to recognize that we were gaining a
broad and unique perspective on process and innovation in the federal
bureaucracy. Our research offered a rare opportunity for a detailed
examination of agency decision making and its effects. ETIP, moreover,
emerged in our study as a program with a potentially powerful impact
on the federal government. Though all the implications of our data
have not yet been explored, some preliminary conclusions can be made
about the nature of the American bureaucracy, the process of public
policy change, and their relationship to the way in which ETIP
operates.

An understanding of ETIP must begin with an examination of the
program's place in the federal bureaucracy. ETIP is located at the
National Bureau of Standards (NBS), part of the Department of
Commerce (DoC), and its relationship with both of these larger
organizations has greatly affected program development.

DoC for example, keeps a closer watch on ETIP than on more traditional branches of NBS. Even though ETIP at first had difficulty developing an active program, DoC wanted projects to begin quickly. DoC also seems to view ETIP more as a change agent than as a detached analyst of technology policy. The program is under constant pressure to demonstrate that it has aided the development and commercialization of new technology or otherwise fulfilled DoC's broader economic goals.

ETIP is also subject to pressures within NBS. As part of the director's office, the program had a rather unusual location at the bureau, somewhat outside the regular "table of organization." Unlike most of the Bureau's efforts, ETIP is not directly involved in "hard" scientific research. NBS administrators sometimes see it as a "soft" program, more concerned with self-aggrandizement and public relations than with science. In addition, they fear that ETIP's politically controversial projects may eventually become a source of embarrassment.

None of these pressures would pose severe problems if ETIP's future funding were certain. ETIP, however, is a new program, and a similar effort at the National Science Foundation has already been scrapped. During the past few years there have been several times when ETIP's demise appeared imminent. Doubts about ETIP's "usefulness" and "scientific value" make it necessary for the program to demonstrate its worth through highly "visible" projects, leading at times to unwise project choices. DoC's interest in practical effects, furthermore, is not always consonant with NBS's concern for scientific rigor. It is thus not surprising that ETIP often vacillates in its emphasis between "science" and "practical value."

ETIP's lack of clear focus is also indicated by constant shifts in the program's overall theoretical emphasis from technological change to social benefits, government efficiency, and experimental methods. These shifts can be related to the third major factor of ETIP's environment—the agencies with which it must cooperate.

In theory, the development of policy experiments is relatively straightforward. ETIP begins by conducting background research that investigates the relationship between public policy and technological change. The theoretical propositions that are developed are next translated into specific policy change hypotheses. Relevant agencies are then contacted, and "experimental" tests are conducted.

Reality, however, is not so simple. Although projects require agency cooperation, untested changes in technologically relevant policies are of little interest to most agencies. And if an agency sees no benefits accruing from its participation in a project, ETIP's willingness to provide expertise, fund "exceptional costs," and assume risk is meaningless.

In practice ETIP begins project development not by considering "theory," or by constructing rigorous hypotheses, but rather by establishing agency "contacts." These can be developed through personal relationships, through professional acquaintance, or even through formal presentations of past ETIP accomplishments. An attempt is made to understand agency problems and to formulate projects that address them. Project "champions" are sought who will support ETIP efforts and identify their own careers with them.

Agencies have agreed to participate in ETIP projects for a number of different reasons. Sometimes they are under external pressure to improve the efficiency of some aspect of their operations, but lack either the expertise or the authority to make useful policy changes. ETIP then becomes a convenient resource, and the development of a cooperative project indicates that the agency is "doing something." Just as important, in case of failure ETIP can shoulder most of the blame.

Even if a project holds little relevance to an agency, some staff members may still find such a project in their own interest. By identifying with a successful ETIP project a person's career may be advanced or his "power" within agency politics enhanced.

Interestingly enough, the availability of ETIP funds is rarely a sufficient reason for agencies to cooperate. Indeed, sometimes ETIP finds itself in the position of trying to "sell" money to agencies that are worried they may be unable to spend even their own funds. In some cases, however, when agencies are unable to apply their funds for particular purposes, the availability of ETIP's money is useful.

When ETIP and agency goals are at least partially congruent, projects can be developed that meet mutual needs. ETIP and the Federal Supply Service, for example, have jointly developed experiments using new life-cycle-costing procurement procedures. ETIP anticipates, perhaps over-optimistically, that these purchasing practices will stimulate the development of more energy-efficient appliances while at the same time FSS will gain considerable long-term cost savings.

However, few such situations have been found, and projects often seem more closely related to agency needs than to ETIP's technological concerns. This problem can best be understood in the context of external pressures that impel ETIP to develop projects and allocate funds quickly. During each of ETIP's first two years of operation nearly a million dollars of its budget went unspent, and within the federal bureaucracy this is regarded as clear evidence that something is wrong. Given ETIP's need to spend money, it is not surprising that it sometimes compromised program goals in order to develop "useful" projects concerned with "newsworthy" topics such as energy, drugs, and occupational safety.

Even after an agency agrees to cooperate in a project, delicate negotiations remain, as ETIP and the agency decide their respective roles within it. ETIP generally provides "exceptional" costs for project support, but at least some agency commitment is desired. This usually takes the form of staff time, with agencies providing day-to-day project managers, while ETIP "monitors" overall progress.

Project funding must also be determined, but as we have seen, this is rarely a major source of ETIP-agency conflict. When necessary, ETIP has been quite willing to spend freely on projects once agency cooperation is assured. As a result, the amount of a project's funding is not necessarily related to ETIP's judgment of its "importance" as a test of technology policy issues. Over time, moreover, ETIP has tended to develop more expensive projects, and has created new program elements that are better able to spend funds.

ETIP-agency negotiations culminate in a formal "project plan" that specifies the details of ETIP, agency, and contractor responsibilities—arrangements for fund transfers, contractor selection, and project management and monitoring. An important part of this is the "work statement" which specifies project hypotheses, tasks to be carried out, and "milestones" for project success. As might be expected, the development of an acceptable project plan is often a time-consuming process.

After funds are transferred problems can still occur. Pressure for change can emanate from a number of sources, including congressional scrutiny, agency politics, pressure groups, and changing ETIP priorities. After experimental policy changes are implemented, results must still be evaluated and recommendations for future action made. Few ETIP projects have reached this stage, however, and generalizations cannot yet be made.

Examples of ETIP Projects

Thus far our discussion of bureaucratic process has necessarily been somewhat abstract. A specific example, however, will help illustrate the factors that affect many ETIP projects.

One of ETIP's general hypotheses is that government regulations often impose barriers to private sector innovation. Confusing or lengthy certification procedures, for example, can inhibit a company's investment in new technology by adding to market uncertainty, regulatory compliance costs, and the time it takes before a product can be sold profitably. ETIP saw one opportunity to reduce the adverse impact of such regulations by developing an experiment with new drug certification. The original idea was to help the Food and Drug Administration (FDA) develop safe methods of monitoring the early release of potentially important new drugs for field testing. If this proved successful, more effective new drugs could be sold earlier, the public would benefit, and manufacturers, realizing greater profits, would presumably be more willing and able to invest in future drug development.

After extended discussion, however, FDA decided that new drugs could not be released early merely for purposes of policy experimentation. FDA argued that its primary mission is protecting public health and that early release of drugs could be dangerous. At the time FDA was being criticized by consumer groups, politicians, and the press as proindustry and insufficiently concerned with drug safety. Thus FDA was unwilling to support a project that appeared to favor drug manufacturers by allowing them greater profits at the cost of possible danger to public health. (It might be noted that it is extremely difficult to determine whether releasing new drugs earlier would be beneficial or harmful to American public health.)

FDA, however, was interested in developing better methods of monitoring new drugs *after* normal approval processes had been completed. In November of 1975 Senators Kennedy and Javits had proposed legislation authorizing the creation of postmarketing surveillance systems. Although this bill has not yet been passed, FDA is naturally concerned that it will have an increased future responsibility in this area. Since FDA's own research budget is limited, ETIP was seen as a useful source both of funds and of methodological expertise. ETIP was anxious to develop an "experiment" with drugs and agreed to restructure the original project to answer two specific questions: (1) Should new drugs be monitored intensively after FDA approval? (2) If so, what new drugs, under what circumstances, and how?

As now designed, this project will no longer result in earlier marketing of new drugs and will likely add further regulations to an already time-consuming process. Thus, although the project is potentially very important and useful, it has little, if any, relevance to technological innovation. Its cost, however, is more than a million dollars, a significant portion of ETIP's annual budget.

Many other projects have been affected by similar bureaucratic processes. For example, ETIP and the Federal Rail Administration (FRA) developed a project concerned with the rates charged for the transport of perishable produce in refrigerated rail cars ("reefers"). FRA argued that the critical shortage developing in the supply of "reefers" resulted from the fact that rates established for this service by the Interstate Commerce Commission (ICC) did not permit an adequate profit on investments. ETIP saw an opportunity to support a detailed economic study of perishable commodity transport that would provide data to support arguments for "fairer" rates. If ICC then established higher rates, investment in "reefer" technology would increase.

The railroad industry's own doubts about the future of refrigerated rail transport, however, led to lagging FRA interest and the project suffered serious delays. Although the envisioned economic study was finally completed, it was out of phase with ICC hearings and has had little effect on either rates or railroad practices.

Another example is a project in which the Federal Supply Service (FSS) is attempting to use noise level as a criterion in the purchase of power lawnmowers. Such a purchasing policy, ETIP thinks, can lead to the development and commercialization of quieter lawnmowers. Lawyers at FSS, however, decided that the agency cannot legally use noise as a consideration in its lawnmower purchases since noise reduction cannot be given a precise monetary value in product comparisons. As a result, the lawnmower project has been stalled.

Evaluating the Program

While ETIP is certainly a useful experiment in bureaucratic reform, our research indicates that the program has become very different from what its sponsors and planners envisioned. Three specific findings should be mentioned.

First, although many of ETIP's individual projects are useful, they are not coherently interrelated as a group. ETIP's need to spend money led to quick, "opportunistic" project choices. DoC's concern for "practical value" influenced ETIP to select "newsworthy" projects, which were not necessarily most important to an understanding of public policy and technological change.

Second, as time has gone by, projects and program activities have deemphasized technological goals and focused instead on issues of policy experimentation and administrative efficiency. A recent internal description of "the need for ETIP," for example, argues:

> ETIP currently is addressing three needs which apparently are not being satisfied by existing federal programs. . . . Firstly, ETIP provides a multi-agency focus for policy problems. . . . Secondly, ETIP operates as a catalyst for change . . . with respect to a variety of policy problems. . . . A third need . . . concerns setting standards for policy experimentation and evaluation. . . . [Experimental Technology Incentives Program 1976: 36]

Nowhere in this statement can any reference to technology be found.

This shift has resulted primarily from ETIP's need to cooperate with agencies that have little interest in technology as such.

Finally, ETIP has vacillated between an emphasis on the scientific testing of technology-change hypotheses and a role as a "change agent" concerned with projects that provide concrete social benefits. This has been the result of conflicting pressures generated by NBS and DoC, and of the personal career interests of particular program managers.

To summarize, ETIP's activities cannot be understood without considering the program's position in the federal bureaucracy and the internal dynamics at both ETIP and cooperating agencies. The program's formal plans and rules provide only a bare outline—a rationalization for what actually happens. Within these general guidelines staff members have developed informal understandings about the procedures that actually work best and the projects that can really be developed. Their actions are conditioned not only by a desire to "facilitate technological change," but also by a more basic drive for personal survival and advancement within the government.

ETIP's informal organization has been affected by a number of environmental factors that have no place in the program's formal plan. Different elements in ETIP's bureaucratic environment had different perspectives about what the program could and should do. DoC wanted action, evidence that improved products were being developed. NBS wanted rigor and growth in scientific knowledge about the nature of innovation. Most of ETIP's agency partners, however, cared very little about improved knowledge or new technology. They simply wanted to do their own jobs better. And, if ETIP wanted agency cooperation, it had to find individual bureaucrats who saw benefits for their personal career interests. All of ETIP's activities, moreover, occurred under increasing scrutiny by the Office of Management and Budget, the National Academy of Science Evaluation Panel, and a number of Congressional committees.

For ETIP to survive, and for its individual staff members to advance, these pressures had to be reconciled. The informal understandings and procedures that developed were, in this sense, adaptive responses. At the same time, these informal dynamics of ETIP operations must be understood if useful improvements in formal organization are to be suggested.

Since our final report was submitted, it has provided the basis for continuing deliberations by the ETIP Evaluation Panel and the Department of Commerce. As a result, there have been a number of recent changes in program orientation that at least partially reflect our recommendations. ETIP has been moved from the Director's Office and has become a new NBS Center for Field Methodology. As such, it has begun to refine its theoretical focus as part of an interorganizational consortium clearly oriented toward technological innovation. The value of our understanding of informal organization is now being tested.

Wider Implications

Bureaucracies in general, and the American bureaucracy in particular, are often accused of inherent resistance to policy change. Politicians as varied as George Wallace, Jimmy Carter, and Mao Zedong have all argued that "real change" can occur only if "entrenched" bureaucracies are avoided or eliminated.

Viewed as a whole, ETIP's projects provide evidence about the possibility of institutionalizing a source of policy change without drastically altering the structure of the federal bureaucracy. ETIP's founders hoped that a small organization concerned with new policies specifically directed at technological innovation could significantly affect federal agency operations. Our research indicates that this hope was both partially realized and somewhat overoptimistic. Although specific ETIP projects have been useful, and some new policies are being instituted, the program has been unable to maintain a well-defined purpose and has been too willing to assume agency goals as its own.

ETIP's movement away from focus on technology has resulted from a rather complicated combination of organizational, political, and environmental factors. It would be inaccurate to interpret our findings simply as an indication that it was the nature of the bureaucracy that prevented ETIP from stimulating meaningful change. ETIP still sees itself as a catalyst for broad policy changes, but its deemphasis of technology has created real problems. A small program like ETIP cannot have much effect unless its objectives are focused. This is the reason we recommended a return to ETIP's earlier focus on technology, feeling that with this step ETIP would increase its chances of significantly affecting public policy.

Although it is true that bureaucratic organizations often resist change, to explain this in terms of the "essential inertia of bureaucracy" is at best a gross oversimplification. Bureaucracies do not operate in a vacuum. They are affected by the political, social, and economic context within which they exist. Environmental and organizational factors can at times retard innovation and reinforce bureaucratic "stodginess," but in other situations they can be stimulants of change.

These statements are not meant as truisms, but rather as arguments that more in-depth, contextual case studies are needed before the operations of bureaucracies can be fully understood. This entails examining the environment within which bureaucracies operate, the relationships among bureaucracies, and the informal organization that evolves within them. Anthropologists, accustomed to integrating a variety of qualitative and quantitative factors in the analysis of particular ethnographic settings, seem eminently suited to carry out this type of research.

Note

1. Other members of the research team included Ronald Cohen, Ronnie Britan, and Angelique Haugerud, all of Northwestern University, as well as a number of additional research assistants and analysts.

References

Britan, Gerald M., and Bette Denich
    1976   Environment and Choice in Rapid Social Change. *American Ethnologist* 3: 55-72.
Experimental Technology Incentives Program
    1976   *Briefing Book*. Washington, D.C.: National Bureau of Standards.
ETIP Evaluation Panel
    1974   *ETIP Evaluation Panel Report*. Washington, D.C.: National Academy of Science.
Foster, George
    1969   *Applied Anthropology*. Boston: Little, Brown.
Hufbauer, G. C.
    1966   *Synthetic Materials and the Theory of International Trade*. London: Duckworth.
Keesing, D. B.
    1967   The Impact of Research and Development on United States Trade. *Journal of Political Economy* 75: 38-48.
Nader, Laura
    1972   Up the Anthropologist—Perspectives Gained from Studying Up. In D. Hymes (ed.), *Reinventing Anthropology*. New York: Random House.
Nixon, Richard M.
    1972   *President's Annual Budget Message*. Washington, D.C.: U.S. Government Printing Office.
Vernon, Raymond
    1966   International Investment and International Trade in the Product Cycle. *Quarterly Journal of Economics*, May: 190-207.
Wolf, Eric, and John Cole
    1974   *The Hidden Frontier*. New York: Academic Press.

6.

The Blessed Job in Nigeria

RONALD COHEN

I first visited Nigeria in the 1950s as a young anthropologist carrying out fieldwork in the far northeast portion of the country. Since then I have returned regularly, four times during the 1960s and for two years during the 1970s. During that time, especially since independence, and despite a costly civil war, the country has developed very rapidly. A good road and rail system now connects all major centers, primary education bids fair to be universal and compulsory by 1980, and by that date there will be ten, possibly more, full-fledged universities. Electrification is moving into rural areas, industrialization and water conservation are growing rapidly, and Nigeria's standing as the most powerful and most developed Black African country seems clearly established. These are solid achievements. No one familiar with the low-income nations can have anything but respect and admiration for the verve, the excitement, and the clearly observable energy of the peoples who have produced these changes in their own society.

During this period, outside scholars have concentrated on a wide range of problems that intervene to facilitate and restrain the achievement of national goals. Party politics, the military, and a terrible civil war seemed more relevant issues than bureaucracy. Recently, however, this view has changed, and attention is turning to a critical analysis of the modernizing elite itself (Dresang 1972; Hyden 1972; Murray 1972; Moris 1972; Price 1975; LeVine 1975). Observers both inside and outside the country have realized that the coordination, control, and leadership required to transform African societies is a major factor in modernization. It is, therefore, a basic assumption of this paper that the very infrastructure created to carry out development is, in fact, one of the main obstacles to its achievement.

In Nigeria, investigations initiated by the Murtalla government into the conduct of affairs by public servants have brought to light massive inefficiencies, nepotism, corruption, and mismanagement. During the last months of 1975, over 10,000 public servants (15 percent of the civil service), many of them in high office, were forcibly retired for reasons considered due cause under existing regulations (*West Africa*, 8 December 1975: 1477). The mere size and scope of such a dislocation in government demands some attention from scholars concerned with bureaucracy in contemporary society.

In this paper I will not examine the effects of this recent turnover— no research has been done on the topic as yet—instead, I wish to ask how and why the problem has arisen in the first place. Quite clearly, the Nigerian bureaucracy has over the years developed patterns of behavior; cultural norms; and sets of shared, learned, and transmitted behaviors that are of the same order as those anthropologists have studied among various cultures around the world. Here, however, the functioning and malfunctioning of the system affects the lives of millions of citizens outside the system whose labors pay for its mistakes and persistence.

The Nigerian bureaucracy is a partially-separate sociocultural system set into, and articulated with, a wider, culturally plural, national entity. In this sense the bureaucracy is a set of new social structures grafted on top of what were in the recent past a set of forcibly subjugated, previously autonomous, African societies. This colonial imposition created its own problems, and its own culture. Many of its major features are those of bureaucracies elsewhere—hierarchical, pyramidal, chains of offices; regulations; and budgeted resources for coordinating and carrying out public services and government policies. Other features are less universal. These involve patterns of overcentralization of decision making, excessive hierarchy, programmed inexperience, and corruption, to name only a few of the most obvious characteristics of the system. These roadblocks affect one another and are, in turn, a function of colonialism; postcolonial factionalism; rapid growth and change; a lack of proper disciplinary and auditing procedures; and a culture of fear, animosity, and cynicism that results from these practices and feeds back to hold them in place.

Maladaptive Patterns

OVERCENTRALIZED DECISION MAKING

Anyone having even a cursory knowledge of Nigerian bureaucracy understands the frustrations of overcentralization. To get a decision about even the most minor matters very often requires getting the sanction of the very top man in the department. If the matter is at all important, it can go even higher. Officials at the top are overworked, while their subordinates are underutilized. In a number of instances, department heads lock all their files if they must be away from the office for more than one day. We were told that this maintains control of information necessary for decision making in the hands of superiors. Subordinates who do not refer matters to superiors are considered to be rebellious usurpers.

Typically, the man on top in an office or a department hands out very limited and partial tasks to subordinates. All coordination, planning, supervision, and decision making go to the center or top man in the department. The system is buttressed by the tradition that officials are held responsible for actions of subordinates. It works well enough, given a hardworking and carefully competent department head who can get his subordinates to carry out necessary tasks. Essential jobs are ultimately accomplished, although backlogs are the rule. On the other hand, the system places strains on officials in top positions and produces a cultural norm which says in effect (1) never do anything on your own initiative; (2) get to the top if you wish to get something done; better still, get to the superior of the top man, and that will make things sure.

The observable effects of this problem are front offices full of people doing very little work, often not "on seat" (not at their desks), and back offices with a few harried, overworked department heads who often work nights.[1]

EXCESSIVE HIERARCHY

By definition, all bureaucratic systems are hierarchical—but the degree of hierarchy varies. Lowest to highest salary differentials in the USA run approximately 1 : 6. In Nigeria, with seventeen separate levels of hierarchy, salary differences run from ₦800 to ₦16,000 or 1 : 20.[2]

Twenty years ago the Gorsuch Report (1954) complained of excessive distinctions between upper and lower levels of the public services, distinctions that had developed under colonial rule. As a result, a pyramid of grades was initiated to mask the older ranking of "senior" and "junior" service. Nevertheless, the sociocultural distinctions hang on, supported by different allowances, different leave policies, separate washrooms, separate housing, pay differentials, and divergent general lifestyles.[3] The perquisites of each occupational class are jealously guarded. Not to observe the niceties of departmental or interclass hierarchy creates delay and almost paranoid animosity toward the outsider who forgets, or dares to avoid, the proper procedures (unless connections to influential people are his reason). On the other hand, to try to get something done simply by using the formal hierarchy is foolhardy. As a participant in the system, I found it essential to cultivate at least one "friend" in each department (of a university administration) whom I could ask for news that my paperwork was advancing through the system, and who would help activate the system on my behalf.

The comparatively large number of ranks between the top and the bottom of any job or any department (e.g., seven separate and formal promotions are required to go from bottom to top of the academic ladder in Nigeria) means that advancement within a department is slower than in less stratified systems. It also adds to the centralism already discussed, since department heads have a great deal of power over the success of a subordinate's promotion through direct authority and the use of annual confidential reports.

However, the basic and most easily observed result of such excessive stratification is the widespread, well-documented belief that factors other than merit are used as criteria for promotion (Wolle Report 1968; Nwanwere 1972; Public Services Commission 1974a: 46). That the belief has some support is shown by Nwanwere's (1972) analysis of the Public Services in which he concludes that after several decades of reform it is still impossible to say that merit and competence have a rightful place in the recruiting and promotion of Nigerian public servants. The most recent analysis (Public Services Commission 1974a: 46) notes widespread suspicion that "unknown factors are also considered [in evaluation] such as ethnic background, age, sex, or that the . . . [judgments] . . . are unfair and subject to favouritism, corruption, or sheer lack of competence. . . ." At least, seniority and paper qualifications are "objective" measures. Any other criteria may become matters of personal judgment, and in a system where merit and productive work are not widely believed to be criteria for promotion, these non-work-related factors become emotionally charged and rigidly protected standards. This, in turn, leads to the usual bureaucratic problem of nonchalance about eventual promotion, since simply serving time must lead a man or woman inevitably forward, unless specific charges have been made against him or her in confidential reports.

INEXPERIENCE

To start a new country with many inexperienced men in high posts is not surprising. To turn such a defect into a continuing, self-perpetuating feature is maladaptive. In 1954 only 17 percent of senior public service posts were held by Nigerians. In 1960, at independence, it jumped to 62 percent. Younger men with little or no experience were recruited and promoted to senior positions within the public services. By 1967 over 50 percent of the federal civil service senior positions were held by men under thirty-five years of age; 74 percent were under forty years of age. Rapid mobility became routinized; officials generally expected to change jobs fairly rapidly. The Wolle Report of 1968 noted that the longest that men held senior posts was two years; the majority moved earlier than that. The entire process was and is aided and abetted by a policy of secondment and the granting of generous study leaves in which officials customarily keep one job while they try out or train for another. The result is a public service in which lateral mobility is the norm. Sticking with a program or job to see it through is not part of Nigerian bureaucratic culture. Persons that do such things are considered overly technical in their approach, or lacking in ambition. Studies of agricultural extension workers in Western State indicate that older, less well-educated staff with families do measurably better jobs than the younger, more highly educated personnel, whose primary goal is to move on to their next position, or on to more training (Harrison 1972). Much of the younger group's effort on the job is accordingly devoted to this goal.

CORRUPTION

The problem of corruption is a universal one within all government bureaucracies. It involves two analytically distinct and related aspects— corrupt individuals, and corrupted systems (LeVine 1975). All bureaucratic systems harbor individuals who utilize public office for private gain and misuse power to benefit themselves or others in illegitimate, unfair ways. Corrupt systems are ones in which recruitment and socialization into an official role involves acceptance, participation, and support of corrupt practices for oneself and for others. The significance of Watergate lies in the fact that (1) the executive branch was leading not only individuals, but also the presidency itself toward corruption, and that (2) ultimately, things righted themselves so that only individuals were involved, leaving the system scarred but uncorrupted.

In Nigeria corruption is deeply ingrained into the system itself. Periodic purges and continued reports of malfeasance, plus everyday experiences, have led to a general belief that the public service system is widely corrupted. My students at the university spoke half-jokingly of their future role in government service as the gaining of a "blessed job." They explained that this referred to a job in the public service that would provide an opportunity for rapid promotion and an access to public resources that could be used for the betterment of oneself, one's friends, one's relatives, and others who claim an obligation, or who are willing to become part of one's retinue within the service. My own interviews with public servants confirmed the general view. An official has obligations to networks of persons in and out of the bureaucracy whose good opinion of him depends on his use of official authority for their benefit. The demands of his kin, of his home villagers, and of the life-style of the elite create financial pressures well beyond his salary capabilities. Commenting on this in the 1960s, Andrewski noted that Nigeria provided "the most perfect example of kleptocracy" (Heiden-heimer 1970: 356), which he defines as government bureaucracy in which the use of public office for private purposes is determined by laws of supply and demand for these services, rather than by rules, regula-tions, or the public interest. In such a system the rules apply only to losers, those who through the vagaries of contemporary history are among the few who get caught (LeVine 1975: 46). This does not mean that all Nigerian bureaucrats are dishonest, or that jobs do not get done. They do. But there is much waste, delay, and often what amounts to sabotage of programs through corrupt practices. These have become so common that up until very recently few seriously questioned them.

The Determinants of the System

One political scientist (Price 1975) has used the anthropological literature to come up with an explanation of West African—specifically Ghanaian and Nigerian—bureaucracies. My own writings (Cohen 1972) are cited in this literature to document what I would call an apologist position. This approach theorizes that African society is different, that it creates persons who, in response to highly differentiated societal positions, derive psychological and social identity and satisfaction from social relations rather than from individualistic strivings. According to this theory, Africans do not separate their public and private roles. Moreover, payment to leaders for activation of their administrative and authoritative functions is and was used in traditional systems. Other writers also suggest that African bureaucrats are merely extending into a Western-originated system practices that are or were indigenous to "traditional" political behavior (Smith 1964). In other words, writers using this approach claim that Africans are different; that therefore African bureaucracy is different, and that it is inherently incapable of doing much better as long as the men and women who staff it are members of wider African communities that still practice and revere their own political culture. Price (1975: 301–32) sums up what he believes to be the evidence from anthropology:

> . . . the corporate nature of these [African] cultures creates a situation in which the role pressures placed on officials in bureaucratic organizations

by members of their social system are overwhelmingly particularistic. Social pressure in such societies, rather than permitting the separation of personal roles from official roles, demands that particularistic or personal criteria enter into the performance of official roles. Pressures of this kind come not only from the individual bureaucrat's extended kinship group, which is likely to view his official position as an extension of his kinship role, but also from other members of his society, whose interaction with him is shaped by generalized personalistic expectations founded in the corporate nature of their society and culture. In such a context particularistic behavior on the part of the bureaucrat is, from a personal point of view, highly rational, since to violate social expectations in a society where social relations are centrally valued and in which individual existence outside of group membership is practically unthinkable, would be to court social, psychological, and even material disaster.

I am not suggesting that particularism, group loyalties, and social pressures do not exist in the Western societies in which bureaucratic organization originally developed, as the earlier discussion of conformity pressure and role theory should make clear. But an important distinction can be made between modern Western cultural systems and those found in contemporary Africa. Within the former there exist certain values that permit the generation of social support for behavior that, in the name of abstract ideals and universalistic standards, ignores, or if need be, sacrifices, personal social relationships. The emphasis that Western culture gives to the values of individualism and nonconformity is crucial here. In Western social myth the man who is admired and who receives respect is the man who resists social pressures and behaves according to an individual commitment to abstract principle. Such a man is a "profile in courage."

Although individualism and nonconformity exist as values in Western culture, these societies are obviously not committed to such behavior in all contexts and in all forms. But the existence of such values does permit the cultural legitimation of the sacrifice of certain social relationships in specific contexts. The values of individualism and nonconformity make it possible for social support to exist for the bureaucrat or politician who resists the demands for his personal relationships in the name of commitment to abstract principles and universalistic standards.

The apologist position not only explains, it condemns.[4] "They" are members of different sociopolitical traditions that, when used in a "modern" setting, are ineffective. As long as "they" are like themselves there is really not much hope for them. Possibly. But it seems to me there is more to it than this. I do not quarrel with Price's static, behaviorist analysis *as far as it goes*. Much of what he says about Ghanaian bureaucracy applies as well to Nigeria. What I object to is the implication that the attempt to combine contemporary bureaucratic roles with indigenous sociopolitical cultures is somehow the cause of these problems. African bureaucrats are not necessarily corrupt and ineffective because they live in a changing world and were socialized into societies originally more diffuse than ours in role structure. This, it seems to me, is an oversimplified extension of the analysis of one situation (traditional society) into another (contemporary bureaucracy) with little or no allowance for the variables present in one that are not present in the other. Unfortunately, social analysis is not that easy.

Let me give one simple illustration. Peter Ekeh (n.d.) notes that the executive officers of large Yoruba ethnic associations do not even know all the members personally. Yet they handle their official duties, often involving large sums of money, efficiently and honestly. These same officials may operate in public service jobs with less responsibility and perform their government tasks ineffectively, often dishonestly. Something about government jobs is associated with such problems, whereas something about similar tasks performed for a voluntary association stimulates different behavior. Ekeh (n.d.) notes that in one case (the ethnic association) an official stresses his obligations, while in the other (government service) he stresses his rights. But why?

I do not have all the answers, but some, at least, are clear. Let me present them briefly.

COLONIALISM

The public services in Nigeria were set in place by British colonial authority, not by Africans. This, too, is part of the contemporary Nigerian tradition. Typically, under colonialism, a senior administrative official or a technically trained official would try to graft onto one or more African societies an overarching bureaucracy that would articulate local political systems into a single provincial, regional, national, or metropolitan system of authoritative hierarchy. The district officer, the veterinary officer, the head of the local or regional public works department, and the many others in colonial service worked with numerous Nigerian subordinates who often had little appreciation for the goals of their superiors (some of which were capricious[5]) or for the rules and technology guiding the behavior of these officials.

This system produced inordinate overcentralization, tension, misunderstanding, and corruption. Africans soon learned to refer everything to the white boss; this was clearly the authority structure of conquest. The colonial official, in turn, mistrusted local talent and tended to check, recheck, and recheck again every phase of work done under his direction. Colonialism virtually enshrined overcentralized decision making in the public service. The man at the top—the white man—made the decisions, taught each man under him a small piece of the job, and then coordinated everything himself out of fear of the incompetence of his subordinates.

Moris (1972), commenting on East African bureaucracy, notes that this "hub and wheel" structure can be quite effective under a hard-driving, brilliant leader. The entire success of the system, however, depends on the man at the top. Should he falter, or become lackadaisical in his energies, then goals and programs will suffer accordingly. Furthermore, he is irreplaceable; no subordinate is ever trained to take his place.

The inefficiency, mistrust, and frustrations of overcentralization became part of the norms and culture of the Nigerian public service well before Africans took over the top positions. When they did, they also took over the managerial style of the previous administrators and the fears and tensions of the previous administration. Elsewhere I have described in detail how colonial rule also fostered dissembling, evasion, and intrigue (Cohen 1974). African officials were articulated into this system, yet lived in another system as well. Both political systems had their own rules, sanctions, and rewards. Abiding by both meant breaking rules in both. Not to raise taxes in Nigeria would cost the local official his job; but under the colonial regime he was given no staff, no allowances to collect the taxes, merely the obligation to do so. Thus, in order to collect them, he had to keep a retinue, and to do this he had to use (embezzle if you like) some of the receipts. Furthermore, his precolonial African superiors required tributes if he was to stay in office. To pay for these, he needed sources of revenue considered illegal.

This is only one among many conflicts which pervaded the entire bureaucracy. The main point is clear: grafting new rules and sanctions onto a previous system made for two systems operating at once, with many important rules conflicting with one another. *This meant that under colonialism Africans learned how to live and operate under a bureaucratic system in which illegitimacy was normal.* Colonial officials, indeed colonial policy, encouraged them to keep their socio-political system going, but at the same time to accept political norms that had little or no applicability to the realities of their own lives. The result was a corrupt system.

To make matters worse, all top positions of any consequence were held by foreigners. The regional and national orientation of the top administrators—the stress on integration and coordination—was not only foreign in origin, but was sustained by the foreigners themselves. Thus, no elite cadre of nationally minded or even regionally minded administrators developed. Instead, local groups became solidary entities linked to the national scene only through a top layer of colonial officials. Ethnic and locally oriented interest groups and political constituencies were turned into named segments of the nascent nation with little or no thought of what this would mean for the future.

The race-caste distinctions inherent in the colonial system not only emphasized overcentralization, fostered and maintained illegitimacy; they also differentiated the lifestyle of the elite. As a matter of strict written regulation Europeans were expected to live separately from Africans, "in reservations." Their salary scales were many times higher and their housing was of a totally different order. All this was understandable, since two different cultures were meeting on the same ground. However, when the Nigerians took over the bureaucracy, they also took over much of the lifestyle of their previous colonial masters. Another legacy of colonialism, then, was a set of sociocultural practices and material comforts: cars; television sets; suburban-type housing with servants; trips overseas; and expensive education for the young. Previously reserved for whites, these benefits were now given to Nigerians who could make it to the top levels of the public service.

POSTCOLONIAL FACTIONALISM

Once colonials had helped breed into the Nigerian bureaucracy the twin blessings of illegitimacy and ethnic factional disputes, the stage was set for a postcolonial donnybrook. Leaders took over top posts with little real motivation for anything but self-enrichment and a transfer of as many benefits as possible to their own purses, retinues, friends, and countrymen. This stimulated interest-group activity and competition for what everyone called appropriately "the national cake." Government services and recruitment simply became political plums distributed in return for favors and to balance demands from regional/ ethnic constituencies. People knew what the new rules were; they knew they were dissembling, stealing, using nepotism, and showing a lack of identification with clearly stipulated national goals—in fact, they competed for the opportunity. All this is well known; my point is not to go over the obvious, but to emphasize the less-well-understood fact that the stage for a mismanaged, corrupt, kleptocratic bureaucracy was set by the caste hierarchy of colonialism. The colonial officials were never trained, indeed, they were never very dedicated, to making a viable nation. They saw ethnic distinctions, reified them in stereotyped ways (often helped, unfortunately, by anthropological monographs on *the* Tiv, *the* Ibo, *the* Hausa, *the* Kanuri), and they took on roles as big men representatives of their "tribe"'s interests. The colonial government, then, acted as a mediating hierarchy above the "tribal" level. The job of breaking down barriers they were partly responsible for, of creating identification with the new national entity, of training people to carry out complex coordination and national planning tasks, was not very high on the colonial officials' agenda.

The result was intense rivalry, a civil war, and only after much travail, a really serious commitment to nationalism that had meaning at local governmental levels (Cohen 1971). The intensity of the localism also meant that bureaucrats were—and in fact still are—representatives of their own regional groups, and must, in order to achieve self-respect, use favoritism, nepotism, and even corruption to further these interests.

RAPID GROWTH OF THE SERVICES

Government is the most important growth industry in Nigeria. I estimate that it represents 15 percent of the salaried work force.[6] Government expenditures have gone from ₦758 million (1970–71) to ₦5 billion (1975–76), with an increasing proportion of this spent for salaries and new positions. State governments have just recently been increased from twelve to twenty, and a new federal territory is to be developed in the middle of the country. From independence in 1960 to the present, the country has experienced a number of periods of what I would call "recruitment euphoria." New state governments, new departments, military coups, and, in 1975, a purge have maintained a system in which new jobs, and new positions, especially at the top, are opening up faster than there are people to fill them. The system has never settled down to a normal growth in which the majority of promotions are earned within a particular department. Instead, people switch from one job to another. This requires contacts, paying court to big men of influence, winking at corrupt practices, and constant angling for horizontal mobility. It sustains inexperience, props up nepotism, and supports the widely believed notion that sticking with the job is for plodders, unimaginative and unambitious technocrats. It means that the public service is a hive of activity in which junior officers are constantly absent from their desks, visiting others, paying court to those who might do them some good in the way of transfers, and finding out what is going on in other departments.

LACK OF EFFICIENT AUDITING

One of the simplest and most overlooked reasons why poorer countries have structural tendencies toward inefficient and venal bureaucracies is the nature of their auditing procedures. Nigerian law provides extensive powers of governmental regulation and of access by auditing authorities to all relevant records. However, the job is enormous and the staff small. As of 1973 the Federal Auditing Department had an approved staff of 541 but only 300 hired; i.e., it was manned at only 56 percent of its budgeted capacity. Along with inefficient procedures, this meant that meaningful checking was impossible. Thus, in 1973, there were still over one thousand incompleted inquiries about federal auditing matters in the 1960s. The 1970-71 records show over 13,000 missing expenditure vouchers (federal); in one Ministry alone (Federal Ministry of Works and Housing) there were 2700 missing vouchers totaling over ₦4.8 million ($7.2 million) (Public Services Commission 1974a: 59). Clearly, with the shortage of manpower, many of the older inquiries will simply be dropped as departments drag their feet. Under such a system, there is a good chance that malfeasance will not come to light, simply because regulatory authorities cannot cope with the job assigned to them.

ATTITUDES TO BUREAUCRACY AND GOVERNMENT

Born under and structured by colonialism, conditioned by rapid growth since independence, by lack of procedures to check the spread of mismanagement and corruption, and, until recently, by a lack of organized effort to do anything about these problems, the system has spawned harmful attitudes among its own personnel and the public. We have already mentioned the widespread belief that promotions are not necessarily based on merit. The "Udoji Report" notes that, even though it is not true outside the bureaucracy, the public service is characterized by feelings of animosity and jealousy between superiors and subordinates, professionals and administrators, etc. (Public Services Commission 1974a: 4).This is another reason why men in authority like to have people around them they can trust, people whose cultural and linguistic backgrounds are similar to their own. Given nepotism, patron-client retinues, entrenched venality, and other improper uses of authority, it is a wonder, to this observer, that so much cooperation and goal attainment takes place.

To the attitudes already mentioned, then, I would add mistrust. And once routinized, or culturized, mistrust becomes cynicism. And this, in my view, is the inevitable result of both public and internal reactions to mistrust and venality. Ordinary citizens in and out of government are led to expect that most public service is not a right but a scarce commodity whose supply and price are controlled by market forces and the entrepreneurial activities of officials. Even when a public servant has done excellent service, in private conversation people denigrate his virtues and pass rumors or tell jokes about illegitimacies, nepotism, and other covert practices they "know" of or have "heard" about in connection with his career. Checking these allegations, one may find suggestive evidence for a few, but for most there is no real evidence, at least at the level of public knowledge.

The belief helps support the reality. Cynicism makes the ordinary recruit to public service ready for inefficiency and malfeasance; if and when he is socialized into a government department where such activity occurs, he must become a silent witness.

Conclusion: The Path to Reform

This paper has focused on maladaptive features of Nigerian (and possibly other Third World) bureaucracies. It has done so for a number of reasons: (1) the development goals of these nations and their ability to transform their own societies are in large part dependent upon such social structures; (2) recent theorizing in this field has utilized anthropological notions to suggest, wrongly in my view, that African society and its people are incapable of running effective, differentiated organizations; (3) an attempt to construct a different theory, based on the history and evolution of these bureaucratic structures, is needed.

The theory presented here states that colonialism, postcolonial factionalism, rapid growth, ineffective regulation, and the cultural attitudes that result from the foregoing factors have produced the present bureaucratic system. Obviously, these are, as well, the conditions to contend with in changing the system and making it more effective.

Nigerians are well aware of this. The large number of forced retirements and dismissals referred to earlier is only one of many moves aimed at making the public servant more responsive. Many of those dismissed are faced with confiscation of property and bank accounts. A special investigative bureau has now been set up and an ombudsman appointed to check on stories of malfeasance and to bring corrupt officials at all levels to account in the courts. Auditing procedures are being streamlined and staff are being hired (*West Africa,* 11 October 1976: 2174). A corruption decree has ordained that anyone asking for or furthering corrupt practices is subject to a ₦5000 fine and seven years imprisonment (*West Africa,* 15 December 1976: 1513). Wide press and radio publicity is being given to the specific reasons for dismissals.[7] In addition, more results-dependent promotion procedures are under consideration, and technically trained "professionals" are taking on top administrative posts where their technical knowledge can be used.

Nigerians have decided on serious reform of their government bureaucracy. Through the use of increased punishments for malfeasance and incompetence, through increased regulation and a special investigative branch of government, they hope to decrease corruption and increase efficiency. However, changing the high rates of lateral mobility that enhance job inexperience, and seriously attempting to decrease cynicism and ethnic competition, do not appear as yet to have become actively embraced public policy. If our analysis is correct, the public service still retains structural and cultural features which restrain it from working as productively and efficiently as it could were these problems not present. The colonial past has left its mark. The normalization of illegitimacy in public service and the ethnic competition are real. Informal demands upon public servants are there.

Bureaucracies change, but they do so slowly and in response to internal and external demands. The Nigerian public service is changing, and it has accomplished a great deal. Quite possibly, after all, that change is the true measuring device.

Acknowledgments

Research for this paper was carried out in Nigeria between November 1973 and February 1974 when the writer and his colleagues in sociology at Ahamadu Bello University were asked to present position papers to the Public Services Commission (Cohen and Tseayo 1974). The paper was written while the author was a Fellow at the Center for Advanced Study in the Behavioral Sciences, Palo Alto, in 1976-77. The author is responsible for any of its mistakes; the Center is responsible for the environment of tranquility and intellectual stimulation in which it was written.

Notes

1. Ghanaian respondents feel there is very little work to do in the public services, and that the system itself discourages hard work and dedication, leading instead to time wasting (Price 1975: 200-201). This attitude was echoed by many Nigerian junior- and middle-level public service personnel and seems widespread among university students expecting to take jobs in government. The "Udoji Report" notes, "Many members of the Clinical Class (Ministry of Establishments) appear not to take their work seriously" (Public Services Commission 1974a: 37).

2. See Public Services Commission 1974b: 257, 261. Official exchange rate: one naira = one dollar and fifty cents in U.S. currency (1974).

3. The system that evolved from reforms started in response to the Gorsuch Report is a complex one. There are basically four types of workers: (1) unskilled; (2) clerical and technical (i.e., skilled); (3) executive and higher technical (roughly secondary or technical school training); and (4) administrative and professional. Each class is further subdivided into cadres or occupational roles, and each cadre has four to eight grades within it. This has resulted in a federal civil service with over 600 cadres, and approximately 100 different salary scales (Public Services Commission 1974a: 27).

4. Price (1975: 130-32) has paraphrased some of my own attempts to understand traditional African culture and society, including my use of the "cowboy" theme to illustrate the values of individualism in the West (Cohen 1972). He then, however, applies my analysis of role differences uncritically to contemporary Ghanaian bureaucracy, and that is where we part company.

5. Change could often be labeled "improvements" in the colonial service. But meaningful change was often difficult or beyond the capabilities of young, relatively inexperienced colonial officers. Thus, changing the length of prison garments, or punishments for carrying chickens to market upside down, might be introduced, then reported as "steady progress" in annual reports. (See for example, *Bornu Annual Reports* for the later 1940s and 1950s.)

6. The Nigerian work force is estimated at 23 million (Public Services Commission 1974a). If we assume 20 percent of this to be salaried and the public service to contain 700,000 workers, government represents 15 percent of the salaried work force.

7. It was announced, for example, that 468 public service officials were dismissed or retired in North Central State; 144 for drunkenness, embezzlement, theft, and absenteeism; 81 for extreme old age, or being in full-time private business; 243 for extreme inefficiency (incompetence) and lack of responsible behavior (*West Africa*, 15 December 1976: 1551).

References

Andrewski, S.
1970   Kleptocracy as a System of Government in Africa. In A. J. Heidenheimer (ed.), *Political Corruption: Readings in Comparative Analysis.* New York: Holt, Rinehart and Winston. (Excerpted from Andrewski, *The African Predicament.* New York: Atherton, 1968.)

Cohen, R.
1971   Bornu and Nigeria: Political Kingdom in a Troubled Land. In H. Volpe and R. Melson (eds.), *Communalism in Nigeria.* East Lansing: Michigan State University Press.

1972   Traditional Society in Africa. In J. Paden and E. Soja (eds.), *The African Experience.* Evanston, Ill.: Northwestern University Press.

1974   Conflict and Change in a Northern Nigerian Emirate. In G. Zollschan and D. Hirsch (eds.), *Social Change.* New York: Schenkman.

Cohen, R., and J. I. Tseayo
1974   A Study of Improvement in the Quality and Quantity of Work in Nigeria's Public Services. Paper no. 1, prepared for Public Services Commission (mimeo).

Dresang, D.
1972   Entrepreneurialism and Development Administration in Zambia. *African Review* 1: 91–117.

Ekeh, P.
n.d.   Colonialism and the Development of Citizenship in Africa. Unpublished manuscript.

Gorsuch Report
1954   *The Gorsuch Report on the Nigerian Civil Service.* Lagos: Government Printer.

Harrison, R. K.
1972   Work and Motivation in Western State, Nigeria. In D. J. Murray (ed.), *Studies in Nigerian Administration.* Ibadan: Ibadan University Press.

Heidenheimer, A. J. (ed.)
    1970   *Political Corruption: Readings in Comparative Analysis.* New York: Holt, Rinehart and Winston.
Hyden, G.
    1972   Social Structure, Bureaucracy, and Development Administration in Kenya. *African Review* 1: 118-29.
LeVine, V. T.
    1975   *Political Corruption: The Ghana Case.* Stanford: Hoover Institution Press.
Moris, L.
    1972   Administrative Authority and the Problem of Effective Agricultural Administration in East Africa. *African Review* 2: 105-46.
Murray, D. J. (ed.)
    1972   *Studies in Nigerian Administration.* Ibadan: Ibadan University Press.
Nwanwere, O.
    1972   The Nigerian Public Service Commissions. In D. J. Murray (ed.), *Studies in Nigerian Administration.* Ibadan: Ibadan University Press.
Price, R. M.
    1975   *Society and Bureaucracy in Contemporary Ghana.* Berkeley: University of California Press.
Public Services Commission
    1974a   *Main Report.* Lagos: Federal Ministry of Information.
    1974b   *Report on Grading and Pay.* Lagos: Federal Ministry of Information.
Smith, M. G.
    1964   Historical and Cultural Conditions of Political Corruption among the Hausa. *Comparative Studies in Society and History* 6: 192-204.
Wolle Report
    1968   *The Wolle Report: Training Needs of the Federal Civil Service.* Ife: University of Ife.

7.

The Dynamics of Provincial Administration in Haile Selassie's Ethiopia: 1930–1974

CHARLES B. ROSEN

The inspiration for my work on the anthropology of administration in Ethiopia has come from the seminal research done by Lloyd Fallers on the coexistence of traditional and bureaucratic norms in an African administrative setting. In his classic *Bantu Bureaucracy* (1956) Fallers focuses on a century of political evolution among the Basoga of Uganda. His primary concern is the delineation of the major administrative roles in the Soga administrative system: village headman, civil-servant chief, and administrative officer. Fallers indicates the sort of tension and conflict that existed between the introduced bureaucratic civil service pattern, with its basically universalistic norms, and the more particularistic traditional authority patterns. In his analysis Fallers shows how the civil servant chief, for instance, faces the dilemma of having to reconcile the particularistic demands of kinship and clientship with the specific requirements of the civil service norms established in the modern African Local Government system that prevailed in Uganda. The village headman deals primarily with the more traditional norms, while the administrator is responsible for the full implementation of the modern universalistic standards of administrative procedure.

Fallers is concerned with the tensions produced in the individuals who filled the different administrative positions, as evinced by his article "The Predicament of the Modern African Chief" (1955). He does not discuss the role of the public, or of particular social groups, in dealing with their administrators, nor does he attempt to portray an interactive situation of a total administrative system at work. In other words, he does not interrelate the levels of the Soga administrative hierarchy in regard to any particular case, so that one has little insight into the dynamics of the total administrative environment.

In my own research in Ethiopia I was working in a situation that at first seems quite different from the one encountered by Fallers in Uganda. Ethiopia was not a colonized country, and so did not have a specifically alien administrative system superimposed on a traditional one. Nevertheless, a major administrative change occurred in Ethiopia in 1942, after the Italians were driven out of the country by the combined forces of Emperor Haile Selassie and the British.

This change pertained to the emperor's effort to centralize the administration of the country, in particular to bring the provincial rulers under the control of a central minister of the interior. Decrees were promulgated at that time, and subsequently, whose purpose was to establish more rational administrative procedures. Above all, the emperor sought to strip the previously autonomous local rulers of their powers.

Although the implementation of the emperor's new administration with its written rules and regulations was lauded in an early work by Margery Perham, *The Government of Ethiopia* (1948), and discussed in some detail by Levine in his *Wax and Gold* (1965), no study such as Fallers' exists for Ethiopia, in which the actual workings of a specific provincial administration may be observed. The one major anthropological work that does deal with local administration in Ethiopia, that of Wolfgang Weissleder (1965), who was a student of Fallers, presents a picture of a lingering traditional administrative situation in which, as Weissleder formulates the matter, "[it] is not that old-style leaders are forced by the exigencies of [administrative] reform to play new roles, but—conversely—that leadership roles of modern conceptualization are 'rewritten' to be played in the old way" (1965: 2).

All these scholars were aware that formal changes had been introduced by the emperor, which, at least on the surface, had the appearance of institutionalizing more rational-bureaucratic administrative norms than had previously existed. So in effect one might suppose that some of the same sorts of tensions and conflicts that Fallers had observed in Uganda could be discovered among the local officials serving in the Ethiopian administrative hierarchy.

In my investigation of the provincial administrative situation in one northern province, Tigray, I found no indication of the sorts of instability and strain upon those who filled particular positions in the administrative hierarchy that Fallers had come upon among the Soga. What emerged from my research was a picture of individuals, both those holding official positions, and also members of different social groups —such as farmers and clergymen—who were striving to use to their best

advantage the coexistence of a traditional, more particularistic normative system, and the newly introduced, more universalistic bureaucratic
one.

Fallers argues that stability and integration could only come about
within the Soga political system when one type of authority system gave
way to the other—when the traditional was finally replaced by the
bureaucratic—and that this was the goal of the African Local Government in Uganda. The situation in Ethiopia under Emperor Haile
Selassie, on the other hand, was such that stability seemed ultimately to
be derived from a certain resistance to having one or the other system
hold sway. Although, as will become apparent, there was tension and
conflict between groups due to the coexisting norms in various particular situations, the emperor continually chose to sustain the tension,
rather than ever finally resolving conflicts to the detriment of one group
or another. Resolution, it would seem, was considered, potentially, the
more disruptive alternative.

In terms of the well-known Weberian distinction between patrimonial and bureaucratic administration, the system created by Haile
Selassie became solidified somewhere between the two types, rather than
evolving from one to the other. As mentioned, after 1941 the emperor's
major problem was to curb the autonomous power of the provincial
governors. This he accomplished by establishing a centralized bureaucracy aimed at ending the governors' feudal prerogatives. Perham refers
in detail to the Decree of 1942 in which the emperor issued the new
bureaucratic regulations for provincial administration:

> One thing stands out above all others in this decree. It aims at the final
> destruction of the old provincial government, sweeping away all that most
> European observers describe, not quite exactly, as feudal in the former
> position of the rulers of the provinces. This process had begun many years
> earlier and was carried a long way in much of Ethiopia during the first part
> of Haile Selassie's reign. But here for the first time, by full legal definition,
> nearly all of the attributes of power possessed by the provincial ruler
> through almost the whole of Ethiopian history are shorn away . . . he has
> lost his private army; he now loses his right to appoint his own hierarchy of
> provincial officials or to recruit his own police. His control of provincial
> tribute is taken from him and instead he becomes, in effect, the chief
> accountant for the government. He is to be assisted, which means that he
> will be watched and checked, by other important officials appointed by the
> Emperor and responsible to their several ministers at the capital. He and all
> these officers are to be attached directly to Addis Ababa by the payment of
> their salaries from the central treasury. [1948: 349]

By creating a centralized bureaucracy the emperor solved the
problem of how to maintain control over his administrative agents. At

the same time he refused to relinquish his prior, more personalistic or patrimonial type of administration. He continued to rely upon personally loyal "spies" to inform upon the decision-making activities of his appointed provincial officials; he also sustained his own potential role as final arbitrator in any sort of dispute, so that he might intervene personally in an administrative case if and when he so desired.

At the same time that the emperor relied upon the simultaneous existence of aspects of bureaucratic and patrimonial administration, other groups learned to adjust accordingly, pushing for the particular style of decisions that most suited their interests in the cases they brought before their administrative officials. Struggles broke out between various status groups; farmers who sought the support of the newly implemented regulations, such as ones specifying the exact amount and kind of taxes that could be levied, came into conflict with clergy and local administrators who insisted that traditional levies and impositions also had to be paid.

While other authors who have written recent accounts of the government of Ethiopia—such as Markakis (1974), Gilkes (1975), and Hiwet (1975)—have been aware of the "contradictions" that existed between what they refer to generally as the traditional feudal order and the ideals of a modernized state, none has had firsthand data on the kinds of nonviolent struggles and conflicts that occurred within any single administrative arena.

In my discussion of administration in Ethiopia I am going to present in some detail an account of the issues in two cases that typify the dynamics of the administrative situation that arose during the reign of Emperor Haile Selassie. The setting for the events is the province of Tigray, where one of the cases took place over the course of forty years, the other over almost a decade. By providing translations of the major official documents of each of these cases, I shall supply an inside view of how the administrative system worked with its combination of bureaucratic and patrimonial elements. I shall indicate the dynamics of situations in which letters and official orders moved up and down the administrative pipeline, so to speak, being interpreted and reinterpreted in a variety of ways at different levels of the administrative hierarchy. I shall also reveal the dynamic relations that existed between and among various groups, and between members of these groups and a variety of officials in the administrative hierarchy, from the emperor to the lowest-level officeholder in the entire provincial system.

The Setting

In Ethiopia when one speaks of Tigray there are two possible referents. The most obvious is one of the fourteen provinces of the present-day

Empire, which, along with the province of Eritrea, constitutes the northern region of the Ethiopian highlands. The other is more specifically the north-central (and sometimes western) region of the province, composed of the areas of Adwa and Axum. These latter two are now the names of two of the eight subprovinces, or *awrajas,* of the province, or *teklay ghizat,* of Tigray. The Adwa-Axum region once constituted the cultural and political core area of Ethiopia, or, as it was often called, the Axumite Kingdom.

What is today known as Tigray Province was the foremost region to which immigrants from South Arabia came, in a succession of waves, during the first two millennia B.C. (cf. Levine 1974). The immigrants, who are generally considered to have been Semitic-speaking peoples, intermingled with the indigenous Cushitic-speaking peoples of the Tigrean plateau, initially in a series of locales extending from the Red Sea coast through parts of the present province of Eritrea, as far as the site known as Yeha, which is found near the center of the subprovince of Adwa. The immigrants seem to have organized a major settlement at Yeha, where excavations have uncovered a temple and other ruins dating from the fifth century B.C., as well as a variety of stone blocks inscribed with an Afro-Asiatic or Semitic language, often called Sabaen, which stems from certain parts of South Arabia. The civilization blossomed most spectacularly in the region of Axum, located some fifty kilometers to the west of Yeha, where the Kingdom of Axum flourished from the first to the sixth centuries A.D. The language the Axumites came to use, known as Gɨ'ɨz, is derived from the original Sabaen. This language, still the liturgical language of Ethiopia, is ancestral to Tigrigna, the language now spoken in the entire province of Tigray as well as in most parts of Eritrea.

The Axumite kings expanded their empire in all directions as they successfully waged many wars. In the early part of the fourth century A.D. the Axumite Kingdom, or at least its reigning monarch, was converted to Monophysite Coptic or Orthodox Christianity. From that time on-wards, even after Axum declined—the political center of the empire moving southward to be taken up by the Amhara people—the traditions of the monarch and of the state religion, as they had been developed in Axum, remained. They survived until 1974 as the dominant institutions of Ethiopia.

The Geography and Agriculture of Tigray Province

As it stands today Tigray Province covers an area of 65.9 thousand square kilometers, and has a population variously estimated to be anywhere from two to three million people.

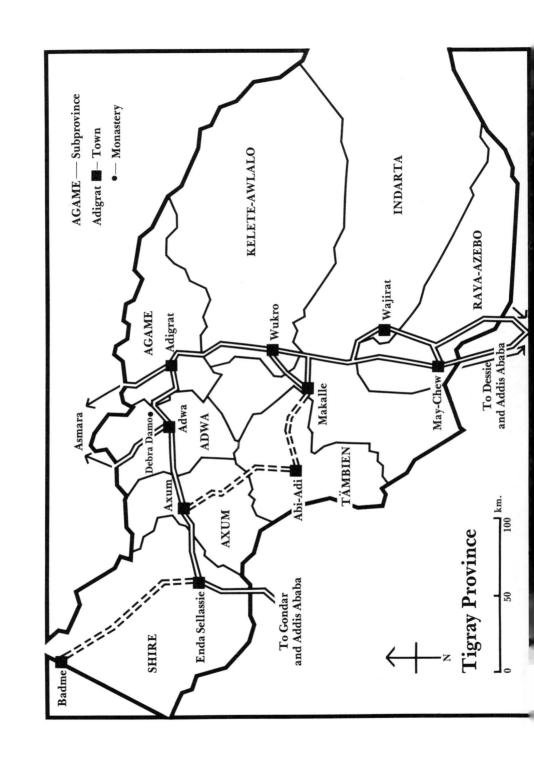

AGAME — Subprovince
Adigrat ■ — Town
● — Monastery

KELETE-AWLALO

INDARTA

RAYA-AZEBO

AGAME
Adigrat

Wukro

Wajirat

Asmara

Debra Damo ●
Adwa
ADWA

Makalle

May-Chew

To Dessie
and Addis Ababa

Axum

Abi-Adi

TÄMBIEN

AXUM

SHIRE

Enda Sellassie

To Gondar
and Addis Ababa

Badme

km.

0   50   100

N

Tigray Province

The bulk of the province is formed by a high, mountainous plateau, although at least a third of the total area is in a hot, inhospitable, lowland depression which plunges at places to 100 meters below sea level. The plateau, mainly of an elevation of 2,000 to 2,500 meters, although rising in some places to almost 3,500 meters, is gently tilted toward the Takazze River in the west and, somewhat more abruptly, toward the Merab River in the north. On the whole the province is much dissected by river action, which has contributed to numerous valleys and gorges. While the high plateau ends gradually in the west—extending out toward the lower, warmer, savanna-like lands of the Sudan—it falls more suddenly in the east to become the Danikil Depression.

The eight subprovinces of Tigray broadly encompass five sorts of agricultural zones. The central part of the province is a wide highland area that extends from the northern part of the southernmost subprovince of Raya-Azebo through the western parts of Indarta, Kelete-Awlalo, and Agame, and through all of Tämbien, most of Adwa and Axum, and parts of the westernmost area, Shire. The mountains throughout this zone are generally craggy and for the most part quite sparsely covered with vegetation; in many instances they are completely bare. Partly because of many centuries of indiscriminate use, the mountainsides have been denuded of their trees and shrub coverings. This has contributed to wide-scale erosion, so that the level areas near the mountains are often scarred with deep gullies. The central zone is also subject to overgrazing, poor land practices (such as cutting even the few existing trees in order to create additional farm plots), and often rather severe overpopulation. All of this contributes to relatively low yields, at least compared to most of the other provinces, and greatly reduced agricultural potential, although there are scattered areas, especially in the valleys, which are markedly fertile.

Two zones, one in Raya-Azebo and one in Shire, are flat, fertile, and generally productive. Although in the past these areas have been neglected, because of either the scarcity of rainfall or endemic malaria, they have recently become the sites of active agricultural development projects. There is an eastern foothill region, running from south to north through parts of Raya-Azebo, Indarta, and Kelete-Awlalo, which is not very suitable for farming because of its steep slopes and inadequate rainfall. The remainder of the province—the fringe parts of the central zone and the Depression beneath and eastern foothills—is very arid, unsuitable for agricultural purposes except in the special circumstances of irrigated farming. In a few isolated cases several of the most arid areas have been made productive by irrigation.

The majority of Tigrean males, except for the nomadic peoples living in the eastern lowlands, are sedentary agriculturalists, most of whom have access to hereditary lands (*rist*) or else participate in one of a variety of land-share systems of tenure. Farming is done with oxen that pull metal-tipped wooden ploughs through the often rocky fields. The farmers plant a wide variety of cereal crops. Although the specific crops vary from zone to zone, in almost any major market one can find— besides the indigenous *tef* used primarily for making a flat, pancake-like sourdough bread—barley, wheat, millet, corn, and sorghum. A variety of legumes are grown, including chick peas, lentils, peas, and several kinds of beans, as are a smattering of vegetables, such as tomatoes, potatoes, onions, garlic, and chili peppers. There are a few fruits produced, primarily lemons and some local varieties of citrus.

There are large numbers of livestock in the province, estimates running from one to two million head of cattle, sheep, and goats. These animals are often quite scrawny, as they suffer from a general lack of grazing areas, a situation made most acute during the dry season, which in some parts of the province extends from early September until nearly the middle of June. The animals are allowed to forage wherever they can, a practice that adds to the defoliation of the mountainside and contributes to the omnipresent erosion.

In almost all parts of the province there is rainfall enough for only one growing season; occasionally not enough rain comes for even the single sowing to reach maturity; and, periodically, there are droughts in various parts of the province. Nevertheless, the soils of the province tend to be fertile, so that despite the generally harsh agricultural conditions that prevail, the Tigrean farmers continue to survive in much the same manner that they have through many centuries of land use in the province.

Political and Administrative Background

In the three decades prior to 1941 the major provincial ruler in Tigray was Ras Seyoum.[1] He epitomized the traditional provincial governor; he sought to rule Tigray as if it were his personal domain, just as his grandfather, Emperor Yohannes (1871–89), had before him. The Decree of 1942 enabled the emperor to remove Seyoum and replace him by one of his own Shoan Amhara retainers, Ras Ababa, who served as the overlord of the province from 1943 through 1947. At that time Seyoum was reinstated as governor-general and held the position until his death in 1960. He returned to Tigray as a titular figurehead, the day-to-day administrative authority being carried out by Amhara vice-governors, or *enderassie*, governing in a conservative and predictable manner. His rulership conformed to what Perham refers to as the besetting sin of Ethiopian administration:

the refusal to take any constructive responsibility [with] governors of the old school [being] mainly concerned with the conservation of their own power [so that] it would have been quite outside of their range of thought to initiate new ideas of reform or to put down time-honored abuses. [1948: 274]

By the time he was permitted to return permanently to Tigray, Ras Seyoum could only confront and accept the changed situation: the taxes were being collected by employees of the minister of finance; the military was under the control of generals assigned by the Central Army Headquarters; there was a national police force and a working system of courts; and his subordinates, who were appointed by the Ministry of the Interior, could take care quite well of the daily work of the provincial administrative office. In the years before his death Ras Seyoum was known as a kindly old man who would accept the appeals of his people, cry with them over their problems, promise to help them if he could, but for the most part was not able to do more than invite them to his palace for the feasts that always were given. For his closest supporters and his former followers only, he might be able to do certain things: provide an office in the lower ranks of the administrative hierarchy; distribute some piece of land over which he held possession rights from his illustrious ancestors; recommend for pension widows and the aged; or take into his palace the sons of his former retainers so that they might live near him.

From 1942 until 1961, when Seyoum's son, Ras Mengesha, became the governor-general of Tigray, the new provincial administrative system had had almost twenty years in which to take hold. While a few clarifications in regard to terminology and the internal divisions in the administrative hierarchy had taken place, there had never been any revision of the Decree of 1942. The structure as a whole—from the provincial governor, or *teklay gej*, to the lowest "sheriff," the *chiqa shum* (literally, "mud-chief")—was intact, although the judicial tasks of this lowest official had been separated out from his other tasks and given to the *atbia dayna*, "judge of the neighborhood," who was responsible for hearing cases of small sum that arise in villages. The tasks of the governor-general, as of the governors of the lower-level divisions of subprovince (*awraja*), district (*wereda*), and subdistrict (*mikitl wereda*), were geared for the most part to keeping watch over matters of security, seeing that the tax collection was being carried out effectively and on time, and handling the cases of the *ghizat*, or administrative offices. These latter, which could include any cases not taken to the courts, usually pertained to the performance of officials in their offices; the hearing of complaints from the people by accepting their petitions; and the giving out of whatever rewards might be available, such as appointments to minor positions. The Decree of 1942, as Perham points out, aims at altering the role of the provincial governor, but says nothing about any particular issues of local self-government, nor about relations between such groups as the clergy and the farmers; the highest officials and the lowest; the traditional patterns of administration and the new ones in areas such as tax payment, church-state affairs, and landholding.

In order to understand what kind of issues were characteristic of the administrative situation that prevailed when Ras Mengesha was appointed to Tigray, and to glimpse some of the complexity that existed and still does, I shall present excerpts from the records of two major administrative cases with which Mengesha had to deal.[2] One concerns church-state relations, as seen in the case of a famous monastery, and the other concerns the appointment of the *chiqa shum*. Both serve to reveal some of the kinds of problems and frustrations that were endemic in administrative matters at the provincial level during the reign of Emperor Haile Selassie.

The Case of Debra Damo

Debra Damo is the most famous of the many monasteries to be found in Tigray and one of the most renowned holy places in all of Ethiopia. It consists of an early-Axumite-style, stone-and-wood church, and a sizable settlement of stone houses built on the flat top of an extraordinary mountain, located in Adwa *awraja* near the boundary with Agame, whose final hundred feet (of about eight thousand) are perpendicular to the hilly ground below. It is believed that the monastery was founded by one of the Nine Saints, Abuna Aregawi, who came to Ethiopia from Syria in the late fifth or early sixth century. According to the legend, Abuna Aregawi set out from Axum in order to find the place to build a monastery. He traveled eastward until he came to the prominent and inaccessible mountain, which he sought to climb. To accomplish this feat seemed impossible. Aregawi sat a long time at the base of the steep side, praying for some means to ascend. In a dream he was told that a way would be found. And it was, in the form of a huge serpent (*gebel*), ordered by Saint Michael to come to Aregawi's aid. The serpent appeared and proceeded to wrap itself in such a way that Aregawi could climb upon its curled tail. It then crawled up the mountain as far as the lowest ledge, where Aregawi managed to disembark and climb the rest of the way alone. Later he fashioned a huge, snakelike rope, which he dropped over the side so that others could ascend and join him. To this day no one climbs to the top of Debra Damo without pulling himself up on the thick, twisted rope that symbolizes the original serpent that helped Aregawi.

Whatever the miraculous feat consisted of, Aregawi did reach the top, and a monastery was begun. Not long afterward, near the middle of the sixth century, the king believed to have been governing in Axum at that time, one Gabre Maskal, came to see the place of Aregawi. Gabre Maskal was duly impressed, and as a result he ordered that a church be constructed, the design of which is clearly in the style of the Axumite buildings of that period. It remains to this day an architectural delight.

In addition Gabre Maskal is on record as having been one of the first Ethiopian kings to issue an order which provides a land grant or benefice to a monastery. He ordered that the land around Debra Damo was to be the *gult* of the monastery, which meant that the tax from that land was to go directly to the head of the monastery for the support of the monks and upkeep of the establishment. Along with the granting of the *gult*, which in effect meant that the farmers were to pay their taxes to the monastery and not to the government, there was a granting of *rist‡gult*, or what is also known as *qobe mariet*, "the land of the monk's hat." Such *rist‡gult* is land which is the absolute property of the monastery, so that the monks can do as they please with it, either farming it themselves or letting it out to the tenants of their choice under whatever terms they see fit to demand.[3] In theory they can take such land from any tenant and give it to another whenever they wish. In the case of Debra Damo it is recorded that Gabre Maskal provided the monastery with 300 fields (*grat*) from the fertile region around the base of the mountain, which were to be under the complete control of the monks. The grant is duly registered in what is known as the *Wongelzewarq* (Golden Gospel) of Axum's Mariam Tsion Church. Onto blank pages in this book almost all major land grants and land transactions that have taken place over the past 1500 years are expected to be written. What is registered therein is usually considered to be the final arbiter in any dispute over land. (Excerpts from the *Wongelzewarq*, including the grant to Debra Damo, are contained in *Land Charters of Northern Ethiopia* by G. W. B. Huntingford.)

Along with the granting of the *gult* and *rist‡gult*, Gabre Maskal is said to have set up a system of taxation which was to apply to the *gult* lands, which in the Debra Damo area could have been either the *rist* of the farmers or else their *shehena*, that is, land divided equally among all those in residence in the seventy village areas (*got*), or parishes, which constitute the subdistrict. The system of taxation that Gabre Maskal is believed to have established for the monastery in the sixth century was reconfirmed by Emperor Yohannes in the late nineteenth century. This system of taxation was registered in the *Wongelzewarq*. According to the monks, Emperor Yohannes also renewed their 300 fields of *rist̸gult;* moreover, he ordered that 300 be added so that his grant might equal that of Gabre Maskal. In this way the monks claim that they were given complete control over 600 fields (all of which they chose themselves, according to tradition), a situation in effect until 1927 by the Ethiopian calendar (1934), when the Emperor Haile Selassie allowed them to take 42 more fields. Thus, their total *qobe mariet* is 642 fields, or so the monks insist.

While the monks can demand 50 percent or more of the crop from their own fields, they can take from the other fields, those over which their right is that of *gult,* only the amount that is agreed upon as the *abel* (tax or "rent"). In the case of most monasteries in Tigray this *abel* is known as *hamsho.* This means "fifth," and refers to a tax rate of one quantity of grain out of five. (The *abel* is called *hamsho* even if the amount paid is one out of seven or eight, which is often the case). When the *abel* for Debra Damo's monastery was set up, no other tax was asked of the farmers, so that they paid the monks, but not the government. From the time of Emperor Yohannes until the beginning of the reign of Haile Selassie, the total tax or *abel* of the farmers in the Debra Damo area, which they paid to the monks, was for the most part (there may have been small variations among the different *got*) as follows: (1) 1 out of every 8 cups of all grains harvested; (2) 1 *chan* (8 quintals or 800 kilos) of grapes and one *chan* of incense in total from all the farmers; (3) $2 from every household head (the number of whom could be from 3,000 to 10,000 for the monk's hat (*qobe*); (4) 12 *chan* of wheat in total for the monk's "wafer" (*maba'a*); (5) 1 *chan* of grain from every village; (6) 25 *chan* of grain as *qufaro* (food for animals); (7) 8 *kuna* (40 Menelik cupfuls) of grain from each farmer; (8) 512 *kulaba* (hornfuls) of honey; (9) 30 cups for meat; (10) 4 *madiga* (1 quintal or 100 kilos) of neug oil for lamps; (11) 12 *chan* of flour for the *teskar* (memorial service) of Abuna Aregawi.

Before the twentieth century such a system of taxation provided handsomely for the monks; many of the monasteries, like Debra Damo, were renowned for their affluence and the splendor of their religious paraphernalia. One can assume that the farmers took seriously their obligations for the support of a monastery such as Debra Damo, especially when the tributes demanded by powerful governors from other farmers may have equalled or exceeded the amounts paid to the monks. In the early years of the twentieth century some attempt was made to introduce government taxation on all lands. When the local governors were able to enforce this, they would be taking grains from farmers who were also paying their *abel* to the *gultenya,* or holders of the *gult.* In a place such as Debra Damo, with its plethora of taxes, any additional ones were bound to be extraordinarily burdensome to the farmers. A reaction against the seemingly inordinate number of taxes imposed upon them was made by the farmers of the Damo area for the first time in 1934, shortly before the Italian invasion of Ethiopia. In that year representatives of the monks and the people went before the emperor. At issue were the number of fields that could be considered as the legitimate *rist-gult* of the monastery; also the matters of the elaborate system of taxation that the farmers were subjected to by the monks and of the government taxes that were being added. At that time the emperor decided in favor of the monks to the effect that they had full rights to 300 *grat.* At the same time some other fields were in dispute. The monks claimed eight additional fields as their own, while the farmers said the land was in fact made up of forty-two fields and belonged to them. The emperor sided with the monks over the issue, so they gained an additional forty-two fields or *grat;* he is also said to have approved the existence of the 300 fields which the monks claimed had been added by Emperor Yohannes. In regard to the taxes the emperor ordered that some of them had to be cancelled. He told the representatives of the farmers that they could be excused from paying the honey, the cows, the oil, and the flour for the *tezkar* of Aregawi, but that they must pay the rest directly to the monks. They were also to be responsible for any government taxes that might be assessed.

The conflict between the farmers of the Debra Damo area and the monks became an administrative dispute almost forty years ago. It is impossible to present all of the details of it, but I can offer some of the highlights, mainly ones recorded in the letters and petitions which fill the administrative dossiers on the case. A major factor in the ongoing case pertains to the system of taxation which the emperor introduced shortly after the Italians were driven out of Ethiopia. In November 1944 a new land-tax proclamation was issued in the *Negarit Gazeta,* which is the official administrative digest. With this proclamation it was announced that henceforth the only taxes that could be legally collected were those due to the government, whose officers would do the collecting. All taxes were to be paid in money, not in kind; any other sort of taxes were thereafter to be considered as legally void. The government would collect the taxes on all lands; where there were *gult* rights, one-third of the land tax (*asrat*) would be returned by the minister of finance directly to the *gultenya.* Although it is not formally expressed, the emperor is said to have stated that in regard to the *abel* or *hamsho* of churches and monasteries, if according to custom, and to their own thoughts on the matter, farmers wished to pay it for the support of the clergy, then they could continue to do so, but without any legal obligation.

In June of 1945, seven months after the emperor's proclamation, a farmer from the Damo area wrote a petition to the Adwa *awraja* governor on behalf of the people of the area. He notified the governor that while the people were paying *asrat* tax to the government, the monks were also forcing them to pay grains to them and also $2 from every farmer. The monks could force the people because the head of the monastery was the judge over local cases and also because the *meslenie* or district governor was supporting the monks by sending *netch lebesh* ("white clothes," which is the name of the local militia under the control of the governors), whenever the farmers would refuse to pay. Shortly afterward, in August 1945, the head of the monastery wrote to the governor that some of the farmers who live in the *gult* area of Debra Damo had met together to make a "conspiracy" (*adima*), swearing that they would not plow the land of the monks, so as to harm them.

As a result of the petitions and letters that he received, the governor of Adwa at that time, whose name was Blatta Dawit, called for a meeting with the representatives (*negera fej*) of the farmers and the chief monks so that he might clarify the issues in the case. Partial minutes taken at that meeting are interesting for their depiction of the major position of each side in August 1945. The main points are listed in a series of questions the governor asked, followed by the answers proffered by the farmers' representatives:

1. Governor: Since you say you're paying many kinds of taxes, which extra taxes are you being asked for? Representative: The new rule of the government says we must pay only the *asrat* tax. But we people living in the Damo area paid besides our *asrat* 130 *chan* to the monks. In addition they are forcing us to pay 1 *madega* [25 kilos from each 800] and $2 from each household.

2. Governor: Did you pay this tax prior to 1927 [1934] or is it new? Representative: We were paying it, even though we aren't obliged to according to the traditional laws. We have been writing our petitions about this.

3. Governor (to the Head of the Monastery): Why are they paying you these 130 *chan* and 1 *madega* and $2 from each household? Head Monk: They are paying *asrat* from our *rist* land. The people are excused from paying the honey, cows, oil, and flour; those taxes are cancelled. They are complaining about the others, but it is in vain. The case has been to His Majesty and we won it; we have our evidence. His Majesty's decision says that, except for the above, they have to pay the rest.

A number of incidents occurred in the months following the meeting. The Adwa governor was not able to make any decision to resolve a dispute in which both sides seemed able to appeal to a decision or proclamation of the emperor. All the governor did was write a letter to Ras Abebe Aregay, then the provincial governor of Tigray, in which he listed what seemed to be the kinds of *abel* that both sides agreed were being paid to the monastery. In his letter the Adwa governor pointed out that even in one place where the monks plowed and harvested the land themselves, the rest of the people of that *got* were paying the *asrat* tax on the land to the government. He also mentioned the monks' insistence that only they had the right to choose the *chiqa shum* of a *got*, not the people (or the government). (This is an important point of administration which will be discussed in the next case to be presented.) In September 1945 a large group of farmers organized themselves, collected their belongings, and prepared to leave the Damo area altogether. The district secretary sent a telegram to the Adwa governor to ask what he should do, as the people were threatening to go to Shire (in the west of the province) and were saying, "Give us new land because we are oppressed." A month after the people issued their ultimatum, that they would leave to farm in another area, the head of the monastery wrote a petition to the Adwa governor, giving what serves as the monks' ultimatum, the threat that they will leave the monastery. He wrote in part: "Since the *tabot* (altar) belongs to the government and not to us only, we are to come out with our *tabot* and our holy property for we cannot live without food."

The tension and conflict between the farmers and the monks was not resolved in 1945; rather the pattern of future actions on both sides was established. The monks insisted then and continue to do so that they must be paid *abel* in accordance with the 1934 decision of the emperor. If they are not going to receive it, they are always ready to threaten the imminent demise of the Debra Damo monastery. The farmers can always find leaders who stir them into resistance to the demands of the monks, which lasts until the local governors send in the *netch lebesh* to force them to pay the *abel*. The monks are always ready to send a letter to the Adwa governor saying that if a militia is not immediately sent to force the people to pay their *abel* he might as well come himself and collect the properties of the monastery. The case could not be settled at the provincial level; no one, not even the emperor, seemed willing to settle it from the central government.

In 1954 another major attempt was made to resolve the dispute. At that time a petition "from 3,000 people from Debra Damo area living in Asmara" (the capital of Eritrea province) was sent to the emperor. These people wrote in their introduction:

Your Majesty, we are people born in Debra Damo in Adwa subprovince of Tigray, who are now living in Eritrea province. We bear a very heavy yoke from which we beg Your Majesty to free us. We have left our birthplace and our homes, becoming emigrants due to oppression.

The petition goes on to list ten different taxes that the farmers of Damo are paying with the final complaint that

with the excuse of collecting taxes, soldiers are coming to our villages every year, killing our chickens and taking our butter. So we gave what we had to the soldiers, but we cannot get food to eat and to feed our children. Hence we are forced to leave the place and go to Shire and Eritrea.

In conclusion they wrote their personal appeal to the Emperor:

Your Majesty, we, your obedient people, are being overtaxed, while others are free and have their rights. We would have come to Addis with our petition, but we know that Your Majesty understands our problems. We cannot rely upon our governors. They consider people's actions as a sin. Therefore, we are obliged to report our problems directly to you. The governors here are only concerned with their own benefit; they don't try to solve the problems of the people.

The complaints about the taxes were rewritten and sent in the form of questions to both the farmers and the monks, with the note that the emperor had said that the case should be investigated very well by the "very close governors," who would then send back the answers to him. Each side asserted again its version of how much tax was being paid, the legitimacy or truthfulness of its position, and the errors or falsity of the statements of the other side.

However, there was no decision made by the central government. The Ministry of Interior wound up sending a note to the local governor that the emperor's decision of 1927 (1934) must be carried out, that the people must pay the monks; a note was also sent for the sake of the people, saying that they must not be overtaxed. This response put the dispute right back with the *wereda, awraja,* and *teklay ghizat* governors, who from the first did not know what could be done to solve the problem. Six months after the writing of answers to the supposed questions of the emperor, a commission (*gubaye*) meeting was held in Makalle under the leadership of Ras Seyoum with the *awraja* and *wereda* governors of Adwa present. All that was decided at that meeting was that Ras Seyoum order the police to make sure that the people did pay their *abel;* also, that since the numbers of police are very few in Adwa *awraja,* the police chief must order more to go there.

In May 1956 the then governor of Adwa, Colonel Isias, called his own commission meeting for the purpose of once again doing research into the basic issues dividing the people and the monks. After listing the taxes and the arguments for and against them he wrote:

> Even if we want to bring both of these people together and let them discuss it is difficult because the monks will say: "we won't leave them even a needle" [meaning that we want every one of the taxes]. The people will say: "although every rule in Ethiopia is improved, ours is not." Because of this the people are causing disturbances and are dismayed with the government.

The governor then wrote concrete suggestions about which taxes should be paid and which should be stopped. He said that the *hamsho* and some others should be continued, but that the *abel* paid to the church was already too much for the people to pay, so they should not be asked to pay the *asrat* to the government. In conclusion the governor wrote, "Since this research to bring reconciliation has taken a long time, the *teklay ghizat* should fulfill it."

There was no final decision made by Ras Seyoum at that time. The dispute continued with the same recurring actions by both sides up to and through the coming to Tigray of the new governor, Ras Mengesha Seyoum, who took over the office of *teklay gej* early in 1961.

Just before Ras Mengesha was appointed to Tigray to replace his father, another side of the Debra Damo affair flared up. There had always been a certain ambiguity about just how many fields were to be legitimately claimed by the monks as their *qobe mariet* or *ristigult*, whether 300, 342, 600, or 642. In 1960 the *negera fej* of the people of Damo accused the head of the monastery of having taken lands from the people by claiming that they were *qobe mariet*. He said that the monks claimed to have 342 fields, but in fact had only 300. The head of the monastery wrote to the governor of Adwa that one man, Ato Taye, who was trying to run for the parliament from the district near to Debra Damo, had been going around, talking to the farmers and insisting that Debra Damo has only 300 fields of its own, this to win people to his side for the election. The monk concluded that this man should not be permitted to judge in any case between the monastery and the people. Shortly afterward the *negera fej* wrote to the Adwa governor (yet another governor, Dejazmatch Gabre Hiwet) to report that the district governor of Enticho, in whose district the monastery was then located, was partial to the monks and should not be appointed as a judge in the case. At another time, the head of the monastery wrote to report that fifteen farmers had confronted monks, who had gone to plow their own land, with knives and guns, refusing to let them plow. At the same time, there was the continuous problem of the people's refusal to pay the *abel* except under duress.

In August 1961, shortly after Ras Mengesha had taken over his new position in Tigray, the head of the monastery wrote a letter to him in order to present as soon as possible the case of the monks, and most probably to influence him toward the side of the monastery. He presented the land claims of the monks as follows:

> The *negera fej* of the people of Tselel believes that the monastery has only 342 *grat*. 300 of these *grat* were approved by His Imperial Majesty in 1927. Also Emperor Yohannes said: "I have renewed; I have added," which means that he renewed the original 300 and added 300, so that the total *grat* of the monastery is 600. Besides this another 8 *grat* still belong to the monastery, but people say, "the monks took them, they are dry and useless." When the people claimed this land before His Imperial Majesty in 1927, they didn't know the number of the *grat*, but said it was about 42. Therefore Yohannes approved the first 300 as the *rist* of the monastery and added 300 more. His Imperial Majesty approved 600 and said, "Anyone who believes something has been taken from him may accuse."

The response of Ras Mengesha to the claims of the monks and of the farmers of Damo is not perfectly clear, but there is evidence that he made a number of decisions which had their effect on the case. From the above account it is apparent that the monks are very reluctant to let go of any of their traditional privileges, no matter who orders them. (There is a proverb written in the application of another monastery about a government regulation to the effect, "Unless he is a monk, the government [or king] can't order the monastery.") During the thirteen years that he governed in Tigray, the Ras allowed the *abel* to be collected, either because he did not wish to offend the monks (and the clergy in general), or because he was reluctant to change the precedents set by his forebears, Atsie Gabre Maskal and Atsie Yohannes. So the Ras issued orders to the effect that the *abel* must be paid, as can be seen from a letter the head of the monastery sent him in March 1962:

> Since the time of Atsie Yohannes, the rule says that all farmers [*gabbar*] must pay one out of eight *kuna* [1 *kuna* equals 5 cupfuls] and $2 from every household. We did not get this *abel* for 1954 [1961] nor the household payment. The Dajazmatch Gabre Hiwet [Governor of Adwa] had been told orally by Your Highness to force the people to pay us. He then ordered the Enticho *wereda* Governor to do it. But the Enticho Governor did not want to go himself and order the people. Because of this we aren't getting food and will have to go away from the monastery to some other place.

Nevertheless, there is no sense that Mengesha settled the matter. In that same year, when officials went to try to collect the *abel* for the monks, some people paid the *hamsho*, refusing to pay the household tax, while others refused to pay anything; rather they signed a statement, one by one, which read in part: "We will not pay the *abel* to the monastery; the law cannot force us to pay two kinds of taxes." It would seem that each year some would pay and others would refuse, or at least try to do so, with the leaders of the farmers, either farmers themselves or outsiders, always encouraging them to withstand the pressures brought upon them to pay.

The issue of the *hamsho* payment was discussed in the parliament and a bill to end it legally was sent to the emperor, but no action was ever taken formally. The topic was brought up at a special "seminar" which Ras Mengesha held in Makalle in February 1970. The representatives to the parliament from Tigray, the governors, and the officials of many ministries participated in the meeting during which a great number of administrative issues and problems were discussed. In that meeting the "illegality" of the *hamsho* tax was stressed, its being paid due to custom (*limad*) not law. Even though the participants could agree that the *hamsho* payment was illegal and led to misunderstandings between the people and the clergy, they were unable to propose any concrete solutions for it. This would have required a restructuring of the whole system of tariff or payment for the church, which only the central government could do.

In that meeting Ras Mengesha made comments which indicate both the kinds of arguments that the monks (or the farmers) were wont to employ to gain advantage in the case, and also the effects of his own decisions. After the matter of Debra Damo had been introduced, the Ras spoke:

> I know the case very well. The monks and *mahibar* of Debra Damo are saying that Atsie Gabre Maskal gave them 300 *grat* first and that Atsie Yohannes came and said: "I renewed and I added." This, the monks say, meant that he has added 300 more *grat*, which makes 600 including that of Gabre Maskal. When we check the *wongelzewarq*, however, we see that it really says "I renewed," but the "I added" refers to grains not to fields. So I decided according to the evidence. They took an appeal and my decision was approved [this would be either by the minister of interior or by the emperor]. Then they returned and started another case saying, "Some *grat* are large, some are small."

At the seminar Ras Mengesha decided that it was up to Ato Taye, who had by that time been elected twice to the parliament—each time garnering support from the farmers, who expected him to help them against the monks—and who knew the case well, to go to the area, count the fields, and bring a reconciliation. The Ras stated, "We don't want the monastery to be destroyed or stop functioning, nor do we want the people to leave their country and go elsewhere. So we must bring good administration and reconciliation to them."

Two years after Ras Mengesha expressed his hope for reconciliation between the monks and the farmers, and his conviction that Ato Taye could bring peace between them, I personally attended a meeting called by Ato Taye, along with three other members of parliament, the latest governor of Adwa, and the local *wereda* governor. The purpose of the meeting was to try once more to bring a reconciliation between the monks and the farmers. The governor of Adwa told the assembled people that they must reach some agreement, or else the government might have to take some steps to settle the problems. Ato Taye stood up and told his own, and the other parliamentarians', credentials, emphasizing that they were the representatives of 25 million Ethiopians. After giving his speech, Ato Taye made a signal to the others (excluding the Adwa governor) and they all went in front of the monks and the people, dropping to their knees. Each placed a small stone on his back. From this traditional position of imploration all begged the leaders of both sides to finally agree to come to some kind of understanding over their problems. At first the kneeling men were just stared at; the head of the monks even began to speak about the rights of the monastery, as if the figures were not stooped in front of him. One local official begged the monk to cut his talk short so that the men might get off their knees.

The outcome of that meeting was simply that each side formally registered the names of the people who were authorized to serve as representatives in any future meetings. Another meeting was scheduled ten days later, but it wasn't held. The problem remained, and no settlement was ever reached.

The Implications of the Debra Damo Case

In a recent review of *My Life and Ethiopia's Progress, 1892–1937: The Autobiography of Emperor Haile Selassie I* (Ullendorff 1976), the author, Dr. Zewde Gabre-Sellassie, who had long experience of service in the imperial government, emphasizes the emperor's abiding preoccupation with form rather than substance.[4] This led, according to Gabre-Sellassie, to a situation in which the enactment of laws was held to be more significant than the enforcement of the same.

This particular point is vital in order to comprehend the sort of administrative situations that occurred during the reign of the emperor, of which the Debra Damo case is a prime example. The emperor had been quick to introduce impartial administrative regulations (and also legal codes); for instance, that there should be a single tax on the land, the *asrat,* to be collected by officials from the Ministry of Finance. In its form, this regulation would seem a sensible aspect of a functioning bureaucratic administration, such as the emperor asserted that he wished to provide for his country.

In fact the emperor sought a separate kind of administration, one neither fully bureaucratic nor traditional. He seemed to achieve his purposes in Ethiopia by supporting the simultaneous existence of conflicting normative orders from which he could choose as he saw fit in any particular situation. In effect he could appear to please both sides in any controversy without ever resolving the major issues of conflict.

As the above case so vividly demonstrates, the emperor was unwilling to clarify the controversy, unwilling to impose a single standard that would apply both to the monks and to the farmers. As often happened, people did take him at his word; the farmers of the Debra Damo area and their supporters kept anticipating that the existing regulations would be followed and the traditional practices abandoned due to lack of official support. As the letter addressed directly to the emperor reveals, people sought to be treated equally under the laws that the emperor had personally promulgated, expecting that at least *he* would sustain them, even if local officials feared to do so, or were too corrupt to care to do so.

Various commentators have pointed out (cf. Levine 1965) that the hallmark of the emperor's form of rulership was divide and conquer. Usually this was seen to mean that he pitted individual officials against one another. As the above case shows, he also managed to keep status groups at odds, so that each would remain essentially dependent upon his favors and his decisions. By allowing the monks to collect whatever they could from the farmers around Debra Damo, the emperor, as well as other officials, perpetuated tension between the two groups. Although some governors did seek to resolve the issue, their suggestions came to nought. To say, as Colonel Isias did, that the monks were oppressing the farmers and that the farmers were very upset with their government had very little, if any, impact on higher authorities.

Whereas among the Soga, Fallers could speak of political "evolution" in his discussion of the processes through which one set of rules and norms came to replace another, in Ethiopia under the emperor that sort of evolution was aborted, leaving a stalemate between the traditional and the modern orders. As the actions of the monks indicate, this stalemate was not altogether disturbing. For those individuals or groups who were either clever or determined, the coexistence of conflicting normative orders offered an opportunity to gain more advantage than might have been derived from either one such order or another. The monks, for example, were pleased to be able to collect both *asrat* and their more traditional *hamsho;* had they not been granted their *asrat* they undoubtedly would have protested to the government and threatened to leave the monastery.

Politically sensitive informants, when discussing long-standing, confused administrative situations such as existed in regard to Debra Damo, insisted that the emperor deliberately cultivated such bureaucratic chaos in order to afflict and oppress Tigreans, whose political sentiments he never fully trusted. The emperor's reluctance to resolve such an issue was linked to his general fear of latent national sentiments among Tigreans; hence the policy of keeping Tigreans internally at odds with one another so as to dissipate potentially more disruptive political energies.

In Tigray culture, significant stress is placed on defending one's land and on seeking vengeance against anyone who tampers with it. The inherent confusion in the imperial bureaucracy as regards decision making tended to deflect aggressive and revengeful sentiments from being expressed against the politically dominant Amharas. So long as Tigrean farmers could be pitted against monks, making neighbors into enemies, both groups would be unlikely to rally together in protest against the emperor himself. As can be seen in the letters sent to Haile Selassie, the petitioners seem to be "brainwashed" to the extent that they believe the emperor sincerely desired his subjects to have their rights guaranteed. Thus, the bureaucratic system itself, along with its civil functionaries, could be made into the people's scapegoat—could be frustratingly accepted as simply not working up to par, not permitting the presumably well-intentioned dictates of the emperor from being carried out properly. Under such circumstances, which might be glossed as "false consciousness," long-suffering Tigreans were apt to remain politically quiescent vis-à-vis the government, especially the emperor, rather than growing unduly demanding or, conceivably, revolutionary.

Church Versus State: The Appointment of the Chiqa Shum

In the preceding section I have tried to indicate some of the difficulties and seemingly unresolvable problems of administration that Ras Mengesha was confronted with from the moment that he came to Tigray. In this section I want to present materials pertaining to the appointment of the *chiqa shum* to areas which are considered to be the *gult* lands of churches or monasteries. This is an administrative issue which Ras Mengesha personally tried to resolve by issuing a number of circulars on the matter. His attempts came to nought, however; he failed to bring about the procedures that he envisioned, due both to resistance to his intentions by members of the clergy and to the misinterpretation or inconsistent interpretation with which his orders were met.

The *chiqa shum*, as many commentators have pointed out, was the lowest-level official in the administrative hierarchy, more or less a combination of village chief, justice of the peace, local sheriff, and conveyor of all governmental orders. It is clear that he was the lynchpin in the administrative system, in that every order issued by the government was always rewritten at each level of the administrative hierarchy until it reached the *chiqa shum,* who was expected to fulfill it. He was the one who went to each household to collect taxes or any other kind of payments; he reported to the higher authorities, most often the *wereda* governor, all those who failed to pay their taxes or to meet their obligations to the government (such as providing food or space to official visitors).

Perham points out that essential as this office was, it was not even mentioned in the administrative decree of 1942. Before that time, in Gojjam, as reported by Hoben (1973), and to some extent in Tigray, the *chiqa shum* held his position for one year only. After the Italians left, at least in Tigray, appointments were made with the implication that they would be for life, that the office in effect belonged to the appointed man, who was supposed to have been a person born in the area (a *balabbat*).

In 1944 there was a general imperial distribution of offices in the provinces; at that time many of the followers of Ras Seyoum in Tigray were appointed as *chiqa shum*, presumably because he had recommended them for appointment by the emperor. Somewhat later there was in effect a general ruling, made by the emperor, that the owners of *gult* (*gultenya*), whether church *gult* or *chewa gult* of the nobility, had the right to appoint the *chiqa shum* in the parishes where they held *gult*. This ruling was translated in Tigray to mean that the heads of churches or monasteries had the right to dismiss a *chiqa shum* and appoint another in their *gult* areas without any intervention from the government or rights of complaint by the former *chiqa shum*. In some instances the heads of monasteries are said to have changed the *chiqa* with marked regularity, leading to the accusation that they were in fact selling the position to whoever would offer enough money for it.

In 1961 soon after Ras Mengesha arrived in Tigray he issued a circular (a letter written by him which is addressed to all *awraja* governors and presents the administrative guidelines or orders pertaining to a single issue; it is expected that the *awraja* governors will see that it is carried out as intended by the Ras) in which he ordered that henceforth no *chiqa shum* could be appointed by *wereda* or *awraja* governors or by the heads of monasteries or churches without prior confirmation by the *teklay ghizat*. He also indicated that no one, neither governor nor monk, could remove a *chiqa shum* without reason. If the *chiqa* had committed some crime, then it was necessary that he be accused in front of the administrative commission (*gubaye*). The first circular of the Ras seems to have been ignored, or at least that is the impression conveyed by a second one he issued about *chiqa shum* in June 1964.

In that circular, which was addressed to all *awraja* offices, Ras Mengesha once again set forth the procedures that he wanted followed in regard to the appointment of the *chiqa shum*. The circular, which has the number 16949, reads as follows:

> A person is given a *chiqanet* [office of *chiqa*] on the basis of being a *balabbat* [one born in the area, from ancestors who had been among the first settlers] and of service. When someone is given a *chiqanet* the *teklay gej* [governor-general] must be informed. This order was given to you a long time ago [on 11 June 1961], but you all ignored this and many complaints are coming to me. This has brought financial harm to the people. It is a pity to hear such things.
>
> So from now on when a *chiqa shum* dies or in some way there are vacancies for the offices of *chiqanet*, the ones who are going to replace them must be given the position on the basis of good life history and service. Each of these must be reported to the *teklay gej* and no *awraja* or *wereda* Governors are in any way permitted to give a *chiqanet* to anyone.
>
> If any *awraja*, *wereda*, or *mikitl wereda* governors do not follow this order, I will take the necessary action. [1]

The implication of the Ras's comments is that the various governors were treating the *chiqanet* as a reward for their own followers. They would try to remove a *chiqa* who failed to conform to their dictates and replace him with someone who would do their bidding, regardless of whether or not he was from the area or had performed any service for the government independent of service to the governors themselves. So the Ras sought to have the appointments of the *chiqa shum* come through his office or to him, so that he might have the final say as to whether the person was deserving of the position. Another result of the circular, a result which came into effect after it was written, was that the *awraja* governors were obliged to inform the heads of churches and monasteries that they too were no longer entitled to appoint *chiqa shum* as they saw fit, but rather that all appointments were to be cleared first through the governor's office. This meant that the head of a monastery, for instance, could only obtain the *chiqa* he wished by writing a letter to the *awraja* governor recommending the man for a position. If the governor approved of the nomination, he would then forward it to the *teklay ghizat* with his approval for the final confirmation. If he was opposed, then the monastery head could not get his choice.

The administrative processes involved in the appointment of a
chiqa shum by the head of a monastery in accordance with the implicit
orders for such instances contained within circular number 16949 can be
seen in the following case. There are forty-one *chiqa shum* serving over
lands that are considered *gult* lands of the monastery of Abba Garima in
Adwa *awraja*. One of these, by the name of Tarahit, had been the
chiqanet of a certain Balambras Beyene, who had been given the
position during the general distribution of 1944. In 1966 the Balambras,
as well as his representative (*wakil*), was accused by the farmers of the
area of taking money from the people. After this accusation had been
made, the head of the monastery sought at least to replace the *wakil*, who
did most of the work, with another man, who happened to be one of the
monastery head's relatives. The *chiqa*, Balambras Beyene, however, did
not agree to this change and refused to accept a new *wakil*. So in August
1966 the head of Abba Garima monastery wrote to the Adwa *awraja*
governor, who was then the Dejazmatch Haile Selassie, that he had just
assigned Haptam (who happened to be a prominent and wealthy
merchant in Adwa town) as the *chiqa* of Tarahit in place of Balambras
Beyene. Three months later the governor wrote to the head of the
monastery and notified him that the *chiqanet* could not be given by him
to Haptam, that it still belonged to the Balambras. It so happened that
one of the governor's secretaries had already written an approval of the
appointment. The Dejazmatch was notified of this and told that he
would have to write an official letter if he wished to contradict the
appointment. He did this, writing that the *chiqanet* had to be returned
to Balambras Beyene. This order was then given to the head of the
monastery. At that point the Balambras wrote a letter to the *awraja*
governor saying that he was old, that he wished voluntarily to give up
his *chiqanet,* and that the monastery could give it to whomever it
wished. The Dejazmatch was again told that the position was to be given
to Haptam. He replied that he would not oppose the appointment, but
had to write to the *teklay ghizat* for final approval. The *teklay ghizat*
secretary responded with some questions about the area itself, and also
with the question, "What service has Haptam given to the government
that he should be given a *chiqanet?*" The questions were sent back to the
awraja governor. He rewrote them and sent them to the *wereda*
governor, who responded to them, writing about Haptam: "The man,
Haptam, is the *balabbat* of that place, and the head of the monastery and
the *mahïbar* believed that he had done a lot of service to the monastery."
This information was conveyed with no further evidence, so that no one
was worried that Haptam was not really from that area. Finally, the
teklay ghizat approved the appointment of Haptam, and this was made
official in October 1967.

    This case indicates that the effect of carrying out the directives of

Ras Mengesha in regard to the appointment of a *chiqa* is merely to prolong the case, as it is sent through the levels of the administrative system and many letters are written and rewritten in regard to the matter. There is no sense that the explicit commands detailing the bases of appointment—i.e., service and being a *balabbat*—are given more than perfunctory attention. Still, it seems clear in this case that the head of the monastery was no longer able to complete an appointment or a dismissal without the prior approval and confirmation of his intentions by the government at the *wereda, awraja,* and *teklay* levels.

Although in this particular instance the general sense of the Ras's circular does seem to have been adjusted to for the most part, there is evidence that this was not always the case. For example, in October 1970 the deputy governor-general (*mikitl enderassie*) wrote an open letter to all of the *awraja* governors warning them that they must obey the orders contained in letter number 16949. He wrote as follows:

> You have to follow the rules of His Highness's Letter #16949. We are getting letters from different places saying that the *chiqa* is appointed and the letters are sent for our information. This procedure is out of the circular sent to you. Therefore from now onward you have to do as the order of His Highness says.

This letter suggests that there is no way to guarantee that the orders written out by Ras Mengesha are followed by all of the subordinate officials in the administrative hierarchy; even after he has written a circular which is supposed to be a guideline to administrative action, he finds that former practices continue. When this happens, then one of his subordinates in the *teklay ghizat* may be asked to send a letter which refers to the order and reminds the governor that it must be fulfilled. If this is not sufficient, then the Ras may write another circular through which he seeks to clarify the matter even further, so that there can be no excuse not to obey his orders. In regard to the problems of *chiqa shum,* the Ras did send around one further circular, one which pertains solely to the relationship between the heads of monasteries or churches (or any *gultenya*) and the *chiqa shum.* This letter, which follows, seemingly created a number of problems in interpretation; as a result of it, there seemed to be a return to appointment practices and patterns identical to the ones which Ras Mengesha had sought from his first year in Tigray to alter.

On 12 May 1972 Ras Mengesha had the following circular letter, number 13244, sent to all of the *awraja* offices in the province:

> When a *chiqa* of a certain place goes somewhere, he has to make a *wakil* to

collect *asrat* tax and to control the security. But now many *chiqa shum* and *wakil* don't obey the orders of the *gultenya* or heads of monasteries. I have received many complaints that these people who don't obey are really obstacles to the administration. Since the ones responsible are the monastery *mahɨbar* and *gultenya,* from the day you receive this letter the *chiqanet* must be administered by the responsibility [*hɨlfɨnat*] of the monasteries' *mahɨbar, gultenya,* and *wanna chiqa shum* [main *chiqa shum*].

There does not appear to be any statement in this circular that in any obvious way contradicts or countermands the guidelines set out in letter number 16949, which had been written almost eight years earlier. According to one informant, who is a governor himself, the difficult phrase is that of *wanna chiqa shum.* This man is certain that Ras Mengesha meant by this phrase, and by the entire circular, that the heads of the monasteries (as well as any other *gultenya*) are to be held responsible for the activities of the *chiqa shum* and *wakil* who are serving on *gult* of the monasteries. The heads must be the ones who check to make sure that the *chiqa* are doing their jobs properly, because, in a sense, the head of a monastery is the "main *chiqa shum*" over the entire *gult* lands. Therefore it is his job to warn, advise, and, if necessary, report the *chiqa* and the *wakil* if he discovers that they are not doing their jobs properly. The monk in consultation with the *mahɨbar,* or governing council, of the monastery may even transfer a *chiqa* from his present *got* to another within the domain of the monastery; but, my informant insists, if there is any evidence that would require the dismissal of one *chiqa* and the appointment of another, then the matter cannot be taken care of by monks. In such cases it is required that the *chiqa* be reported on to the *awraja* governor, who will hold a commission (*gubaye*) meeting, so that the man's case can be heard and an administrative decision be given. In sum, then, circular number 13244 can be considered a warning to the heads of churches and monasteries that they are to pay more attention to the caliber of the *chiqa* working in their domains and be ready to bring suit against any who are found to be lax in carrying out their administrative tasks.

On 13 October 1972, however, the circular of Ras Mengesha regarding *chiqa shum* was interpreted in quite a different fashion. The context for this use of the Ras's statement had arisen almost as soon as the circular had been distributed. At that time a number of the heads of important churches and monasteries insisted that by this order Ras Mengesha had once more permitted them to appoint whomever they, the *wanna chiqa shum,* wished to be the *chiqa* in their *gult* areas. In one case involving the Church of Sellassie (Holy Trinity) of Adwa, a dispute

between the head of the church (*melake berhan*) and one of the *chiqa* (by
the name of Sahlu Desta) of a *gult* area called Legomti, which had begun
in 1967, was suddenly settled through a decision made by Ras Mengesha's
highest ranking subordinate, the *mikitl enderassie*, who had been
appointed in Tigray only a few months before. He, apparently, had the
permission of the Ras to make administrative decisions as he saw fit.
After the *melake berhan* of Sellassie church brought his argument to the
mikitl enderassie, he "won" the case and was permitted to remove Sahlu
Desta and appoint someone else as *chiqa* in Legomti.

The *mikitl enderassie* wrote the following summary of his decision:

> Ato Sahlu Desta in his application said that the *awraja ghizat* has given the
> *chiqanet*, which was given to him by the Debre Berhan Sellassie Church, to
> Ato Amde Mariam Woldu. The *mahibar* and the church said that because
> he is disobedient we have given the *chiqanet* to some other people. He
> musn't accuse anyone. Therefore the ones who have the right of the
> *chiqanet*, that is the Head [*memher*] and the *mahibar*, have said that they
> did not give him the *chiqanet*, so according to letter #13244 of 4/9/64 [12
> May 1972] from His Highness to all monasteries to *assign their own chiqa
> in any way that they want*, we cannot accept Ato Sahlu's application. If
> there is something to be paid by this man to the church, they can accuse
> him. [My italics.]

If one compares the italicized statement in the *mikitl enderassie*'s
decision with the actual letter of Ras Mengesha, which he asserts he is
following, one would most probably conclude that he has markedly
misinterpreted the Ras's order. I asked several other officials how it
might be possible for the *mikitl enderassie* to make such a decision. One
said that the man tends to be emotional, so that when the *melake berhan*,
a man of the cloth, came before him, he may have decided in his favor
without properly consulting the Ras's order. Another, who has had long
experiences working in the *teklay ghizat*, mentioned that there are
sometimes secretaries who wish to exert control over high officials and
to cause trouble in administration, which they do by misinforming their
superiors about the content or meaning of particular rules or orders.
Whether or not either of these explanations is accurate in any way, each
assumes that there was a definite guideline which should have been
followed in order to make a decision in the case between Sahlu Desta and
the head of Sellassie church. When one examines other letters and other
decisions that have been made in this case, however, one finds that in the
past there have been a number of decisions just like the *mikitl
enderassie*'s, that is, decisions that seem to misinterpret or contradict the
relevant order of Ras Mengesha. Although the various letters pertaining
to this case suggest the variety of interests and conflicts that can enter

into a dispute over a *chiqanet,* they do not reveal any consistent use of administrative procedures or of rules that would be applicable to *chiqa* cases in general.

In the case of Sahlu Desta, at times the state supported him against the wishes of the church, and at other times it is clear that the involved officials decided in favor of Sellassie, even when it seems as if the decision contradicted the orders of Ras Mengesha on the matter. As many of the arguments in this case are found in written applications, the normal vehicle used in the process of administration, it is difficult to discern everyone's real interests or intentions. In the final case I shall consider, which involves the Abba Garima Monastery, the real interest of the monks is not mentioned in the applications, but from the nature of the correspondence it seems that they seek to assert their prerogatives, while the *awraja* governor, as representative of the government, tries to maintain the authority of the administration, at least in regard to the appointment of *chiqa shum.*

Six days after the *mikitl enderassie* had made his decision in favor of Sellassie Church, so that the *melake berhan* and the *mahibar* were given the power to assign a *chiqa* in any way that they wished, the head, or *memher,* of Abba Garima monastery and the *mahibar* wrote a long application to the Adwa *wereda* governor, Kenyazmatch Haile Sellassie, which begins, "We of the Abba Garima monastery were giving the *atbia danyanet* and *chiqanet* to the one whom we wanted." The letter goes on to discuss the appointments of two men in 1959 as *atbia danya* in *got* which are part of the *gult* area of the monastery. The two are accused of having left their jobs, having been thinking for themselves and not for the monastery. One of the men is accused of having told the people not to pay the *hamsho,* and of not paying the required *abel* or tax to the monks.[5] The letter continues:

> So these people don't obey us and don't do their job properly. We are asking you to dismiss these people from their *atbia danyanet* so that Memher Gabre Hiwet, who was *mikitl wereda* governor of Abba Garima, can take the *atbia danyanet.* We have all voted for him.

The man whom the letter asks to be made *atbia* is the present head of the monastery. The request was quickly agreed to by the *wereda* governor, Kenyazmatch Haile Sellassie, who sent the monks' letter two days later to then *awraja* governor Ato Aram, as if he wanted to help the *memher* to gain the appointment. He wrote a note along with the letter which said, "We approve of the *mahibar* appointing its own *atbia* and are expecting your approval." Eleven days later, on 1 November, Ato Aram replied to the *wereda* governor by making two points:

(1) When *chiqa shum* aren't obeying or doing their jobs properly, you should report them to us and we can dismiss them; (2) *atbia danya* belong to the monastery and they have to obey the monastery and give good legal service.

These two points indicate that Aram is wary of the Abba Garima *memher*. The monk seems to be seeking permission to appoint *chiqa* as well as *atbia*, which is what the decision of the *mikitl enderassie* should have permitted. Ato Aram, however, is not accepting the *enderassie's* decision as a precedent. Although the letter from the monastery seems to be about *atbia*, the *awraja* governor responds with his remarks on *chiqa* and with the point that the monks can, as always, choose their own *atbia*. Hence there should have been no need to write at all for permission, if that was the only intent.

The monks might seem to have followed proper channels by first sending their application to the *wereda* governor (although for the appointment of an *atbia* they need only to have notified the governor) first of all, but in fact they also immediately sent a copy of the *teklay ghizat* in Makalle. On 22 November the provincial chief secretary wrote a letter to the Adwa *awraja* office in which the original letter the monks had sent was summarized. To this was added the order that the *awraja* office must follow circular number 13244 of His Highness in regard to the case, which means that it had been interpreted as a matter that did in fact involve the *chiqa shum* and the question of who could appoint them. On 14 December 1972 the Adwa *awraja* governor wrote again to the *wereda* governor, saying:

I received the letter of the *teklay ghizat* which says that we have to follow circular #13244 in reference to the application of Abba Garima of 9/2/65 [19 October 1972]. You must follow the circular. If there are any disobedient *chiqa*, who don't do their jobs properly, they must be reported to us, so that we can punish them. If they don't do their jobs properly and evidence is produced for this, we can take them to a *gubaye* and decide.

Although the *teklay ghizat's* letter had made no mention of the specific interpretation that should be made in relation to the circular of Ras Mengesha, it was used by the Adwa governor to assert that the task of punishing or dismissing *chiqa* is one for the administration, not for the monks. This interpretation is the opposite of the one made by the *mikitl enderassie*. It would seem that it in fact is based on the previous circular, number 16949, although the underlying intent of the latter circular could be taken to be identical to that of the former.

After the letter which mentioned the circular of Ras Mengesha came to the *awraja* office, it was rewritten by the chief secretary to be sent to the head of Abba Garima. The Adwa governor intercepted the letter and rewrote it himself, adding several points. He emphasized that it is the governor's right to decide on *chiqa* and that Ras Mengesha's circular must be followed in this regard. It would seem from this, and from other evidence in the various letters, that the governor knew that the issue at hand was whether or not the monks were going to be permitted to appoint the *chiqa*. It would seem that the *memher* of the monastery sought to get official sanction for an attempt to control not only the appointment of the *atbia*, which in fact he already could do, but also that of the *chiqa*, which he had been able to do before Ras Mengesha came to Tigray, but was not being permitted to do by the Adwa governor, even though the same governor had previously supported the right of the *melake berhan* to appoint the *chiqa* for Legomti.

Implications of the Chiqa Shum Cases

By following the intracacies of these cases involving the appointment of *chiqa shum,* one gains a sense of the administrative morass that existed in Tigray, and presumably throughout all of the other provinces as well. There was an incipient bureaucracy in Tigray. The administrative hierarchy and the written regulations—the structure of the bureaucracy—indeed existed, as evinced by the proliferation of administrative levels and codified rulings. At the same time there was an obvious dearth of what might be called administrative competence, or, essentially, administrative rationality.

In fact, nonrationality would seem to have been integral to the workings of the provincial administration. While the authority structure and the authoritative orders had become commonplace in Tigray, as in other provinces, the actual processes of bureaucratic institutionalization—those that Fallers documented for the Soga—did not take hold in a systematic fashion, as they presumably did over time in Uganda. Rules were made, acknowledged, and ignored. Consistency was the exception rather than the rule. At each level of the authority structure, the officials were intent on asserting their own initiative, rather than on a standard interpretation of policy.

In the light of the evidence contained in the above cases, it is clear that very little punishment was meted out for failure to follow orders; at most a letter of reprimand might be sent, but even that may have happened only years after a questionable decision had been made. Knowing that officials were prone to decide on cases according to their own lights and their own personal interests, individuals such as Sahlu Desta were aware of the potential benefits to be derived from persistence in their appeals, for a decision made at one level could often be

overturned at another. Since decisions could so easily be lost or
forgotten, there was an incentive to revive old cases and to keep pressing
for a position, such as the monks' right to appoint *chiqa shum,* even
when an authoritative decision would seem already to have been issued.[6]

Conclusion

The data from Tigray province indicate that the emperor did accomplish his primary administrative goal, which was to centralize his
empire, and to curb the dangerously autonomous power of the
provincial governors. In regard to his attempt to provide a working
administrative bureaucracy to handle the affairs of the people, it would
appear that he lacked a real intention to ensure that the system he created
would actually function beyond the minimal level of maintaining peace
and order and making sure that the taxes were collected. The emperor
did not deliberately ensure that his new system, and the rulings he
issued, would be implemented so as to replace what had gone before in
regard to crucial administrative problems.

Most likely, the provincial administration would not have become
more effective, more rationalized, had the emperor remained in power,
despite the modest efforts of officials such as Ras Mengesha to see that
administrative policies were followed and that pressing problems were
dealt with at least sporadically. The laxity in the system, along with the
superabundance of opportunities for idiosyncratic decision making,
made the imperial bureaucracy ill-suited for any sort of precise, legal-
rational guidelines.

With the emperor gone and a totally new regime in power, it is
conceivable that the one way to solve the dilemmas of administration
posed by cases such as that of Debra Damo has come into effect—to alter
totally the foundation of the system itself, replacing the former officials
of the imperial administration with politically-conscious personnel
trained in carrying out roles in a bureaucratic fashion.

While I have very little information about the present provincial
administration in Tigray or in other parts of Ethiopia, I would guess
that many of the same problems exist, with the emperor's legacy
surviving in the form of a system built around a combination of
traditional, quasi-bureaucratic, and now socialistic norms.

Notes

1. *Ras* was the highest title granted by the emperor, and it was traditionally
   given to those provincial lords who led armies into battle.

2. The events of these cases will be presented as they occurred up through the end of my fieldwork in 1972. In part the present tense is used, even though the situations may now be altered due to the demise of the emperor and his imperial system.

3. *Gult* and *rist* are the names for two types of landholding arrangements. *Gult* refers to land which has been given as a benefice, usually in reward for service to the emperor. Any land can be considered as *gult* to the extent that the tax or a portion of the crop is paid to someone other than to the government. *Rist* is the name given to land which is used by farmers who have inherited *rist*, or land-use rights. Although *rist* is not private property—in fact all *rist* belongs to a descent group, or corporation, and is inherited ambilineally (cf. Hoben 1973)—each *rist* holder, or *ristenya*, treats his *rist* as his own land during his lifetime, and is usually willing to fight to the death to protect it. The notion of *rist·igult* refers to land that has been taken away from the *ristenya* and given in perpetuity to an institution or to a noble personage.

4. The review, untitled, was given to me by Dr. Zewde Gabre-Sellassie, and has not yet been published.

5. This point is interesting because it refers to the job of a *chiqa shum,* that of *abel* collection, even though the letter states that the man is an *atbia.* As will be seen, the letter was responded to as if the man in question were a *chiqa.*

6. It is interesting to note that in a basically authoritarian system of administration, subservient following of superiors' orders did not prevail, nor were superiors feared in any noticeable fashion.

References

Fallers, L. A.
  1955   *The Predicament of the Modern African Chief: An Instance from Uganda. American Anthropologist* 57: 290–305.
  1956   *Bantu Bureaucracy.* Chicago: University of Chicago Press. Reprinted in paperback in 1965.
Gabre-Sellassie, Z.
  n.d.   Review of E. Ullendorff (ed. and trans.), *My Life and Ethiopia's Progress, 1892–1937.* Unpublished ms.
Gilkes, P.
  1975   *The Dying Lion: Feudalism and Modernization in Ethiopia.* London: Julian Friedmann.
Hiwet, A.
  1975   *Ethiopia: From Autocracy to Revolution.* Review of African Political Economy, Occasional Publication no. 1. London: Merlin Press.
Hoben, A.
  1973   *Amhara Land Tenure: The Dynamics of Cognatic Descent in Ethiopia.* Chicago: University of Chicago Press.
Huntingford, G. W. B.
  1965   *Land Charters of Northern Ethiopia.* Addis Ababa: Institute of Ethiopian Studies.
Imperial Ethiopian Government
  1942–
  1974   *Negarit Gazeta.*

Levine, D.
   1965   *Wax and Gold*. Chicago: University of Chicago Press.
   1974   *Greater Ethiopia: The Evolution of a Multiethnic Society*. Chicago: University of Chicago Press.
Markakis, J.
   1974   *Ethiopia: Anatomy of a Traditional Polity*. London: Oxford University Press.
Perham, M.
   1969   *The Government of Ethiopia*. Evanston, Ill.: Northwestern University Press. (Originally published in 1948.)
Ullendorff, E. (trans. and ed.)
   1976   *My Life and Ethiopia's Progress, 1892–1937: The Autobiography of Emperor Haile Selassie I*. London: Oxford University Press.
Weissleder, W.
   1965   The Political Ecology of Amhara Domination. Unpublished doctoral dissertation, University of Chicago.

8.

Bureaucracy and Antibureaucracy in the People's Republic of China

MARTIN KING WHYTE

Contemporary China is a society of contrasts and conflicting impressions. Perhaps nowhere is this more true than in regard to the question of bureaucracy. China is of course not a typical developing society, and she has a longer continuous bureaucratic tradition than any other society. Max Weber's seminal writings on bureaucracy (especially Weber 1968) were informed by his analysis of Chinese bureaucratic institutions and by comparisons with those in the West. But what has occurred in the development of bureaucratic forms in China since 1949 is not always clear to the outsider. In the 1950s many studies of China portrayed it as a society with a form of bureaucratic totalitarianism even more extreme than the Soviet version. More recent descriptions sometimes paint a quite different picture. China emerges in these descriptions as a fiercely antibureaucratic society which uses a variety of means to counteract the rigidities, red tape, and elitism of Chinese organizations and to give the masses—those at the bottom of these organizations—some degree of control over their operation.[1]

It is the contention of this paper that neither of these views is entirely right or wrong. Rather, we have here a situation something like that of two astigmatics, one with a grasp on the tail of an elephant, the other with a hold on the trunk, each trying to describe the nature of the beast in between. We hope to give a more rounded picture of that beast here. The seemingly contradictory impulses and trends stem, in our view, from the discomfort with which Chinese elites, particularly the "Maoists" among them, have tried to work within their Leninist form of socialism. Conclusive statements may be difficult, however, since our beast is also moving—the mix of bureaucratic and antibureaucratic impulses has shifted over time, and these shifts have accelerated since the death of Mao Zedong.

Let us look first at the bureaucratic side of things (the reader may decide whether this is the trunk or the tail). Developments in China since 1949 conform very much to the observations made by Weber (in 1913, before the Bolshevik revolution) about the organizational consequences of socialism:

> Only by reversion in every field—political, religious, economic, etc.—to small-scale organization would it be possible to any considerable extent to escape bureaucracy's influence. . . . Socialism would, in fact, require a still higher degree of formal bureaucratization than capitalism. [Weber 1968: 224–25]

The reasons should be obvious. Even the degree of concentration of power represented by monopoly capitalism cannot approach that which occurs when private control over capital, means of communication, education, housing, and other resources is replaced by state or collective control. Instead of relying on market mechanisms, however distorted by monopolistic forces, to allocate resources, socialism institutes centralized planning and price setting. But there are socialisms and then there are socialisms. The version the Chinese set out to establish after 1949 was based upon Leninist-Stalinist policies and models, and because of this the forces for bureaucratization were greater than they would have been under some form of democratic socialism. Under the Leninist-Stalinist form an elite, hierarchical Communist Party organization plays a leading role in every institution in society. Internally, the party operates on principles of democratic centralism, and in practice the centralist element is always primary, since these principles require that, once policies have been set by the party leadership, they must be unquestioningly obeyed and implemented by all lower-level party organizations and members. (The democratic element comes in mainly before policies have been set, which does not seem to be very often.)

So after 1949 China set out on a course of massive bureaucratization. For the new leaders to administer a society with the world's largest population they carried out a major campaign to recruit new party and state cadres (leaders and salaried personnel). A comparison can be made of the number of government officials and functionaries in Nationalist China just prior to the Communists' victory (Kao 1971: 98–99), and the increase in the number of "state cadres" since 1949 (Funnell 1971: 6). (These figures leave out administrative personnel serving outside of formal governmental organs.)

1948	*1949*	*1952*	*1955*	*1958*
2,000,000	720,000	3,310,000	5,270,000	7,920,000

The comparison is admittedly highly inexact, but it does provide one indication of the growth of bureaucracy after 1949.

The Chinese Communists also socialized industry and commerce and began a drive to develop heavy industry, using as a core in this effort the more than 200 whole industrial plants supplied them by the Soviet Union. They collectivized agriculture and established central bureaucracies to control mass communications, education, culture and the arts, foreign trade, and most other aspects of Chinese life. Once these transformations had been consolidated they established a complex system of bureaucratic ranks and wages. State cadres were organized in thirty grades, engineering and technical personnel in eighteen grades, and industrial workers in eight to ten grades. Most of the administrative structures existing in the Soviet Union were copied in China: the ministerial structure, state planning and statistical agencies, a union of writers, and so forth.

Some perspective on these changes can be gained if we look at particular sectors of the population. Traditional Chinese cities were already more tightly organized than Western cities through the use of local groups to assist the police, as in the rural *pao-chia* system (Schurmann 1968: chap. 6), but after 1949 official structures and controls increased. Military control and party committees set out to eliminate underworld gangs and secret societies and to impose new organizational forms. A rigorous system of household registration was established which has become even more strict since the socialization of the economy in 1955–57. Most housing in large cities has come under the control of city housing allocation offices, or work units, and jobs are assigned by city labor offices. Individuals are forbidden to come to the city to live unless specifically recruited for jobs or schooling; even marriage to an urban resident does not entitle a villager to move in. Grain, cotton cloth, and many other necessities of life are rationed, and individuals not properly registered are not entitled to such rations. Urban districts are subdivided into street committees, and these in turn into residents' committees (supervising 100–800 families) and residents' small groups (supervising 15–50 families). Party and police officials at the residents' committee and higher levels supervise this complex network. Street and residents' committee cadres often run street factories and nursery schools; they conduct local sanitation, health, and birth control drives; they organize after-school activities for students; they assist the police in keeping an eye on suspicious characters and "controlled elements" (politically stigmatized families, parolees, etc.);

they mediate neighborhood and family disputes; and they run regular political study classes for those residents not involved in such classes in a work unit or school. For urban residents, then, access to housing, jobs, food and clothing, and even aid in dealing with family problems or approval for having more children requires that they confront the bureaucratic structures the Chinese Communists introduced. Similar comments could be made about the peasants, who have seen their life as independent farmers or dependent renters transformed into work as agricultural laborers on people's communes, which in 1963 were administered by 20 million cadres—admittedly not all of them full-time officials in the Weberian mold (Funnell 1971: 7).

The bureaucratization of Chinese life has occurred not only in order to give China's leaders greater control over their people. The rationale for many particular changes has been expressed in terms understandable to bureaucrats and social scientists the world over. Larger-scale organizations, it has been argued, can realize economies of scale, pool the resources needed for important social projects, avoid duplication of effort and implement a more rational division of labor, override nepotism and local group rivalries, and so forth. These views can be seen particularly in arguments for the collectivization of agriculture and the building of people's communes, where desires to carry out more scientific farming, to undertake major irrigation and land reclamation projects, to facilitate mechanization of field operations, and to obtain other benefits are stressed. In the cryptic phrases of Mao Zedong, "communes are fine" because they are "big and public."

In some ways the Chinese Communists have fostered bureaucratic control in areas not so controlled in the Soviet Union. The clearest example here concerns the allocation of labor. In the Soviet Union, during most periods, a fairly free labor market has operated, with individuals able to quit their jobs and seek employment elsewhere (although with the loss of some seniority and other benefits, as in the West). Because of this labor market, Soviet authorities have had to use pay differentials to attract workers into demanding posts or jobs in harsh environments. In China, by and large, labor is allocated by the state, and no such general labor market operates. Individuals are directly assigned to jobs and expected to serve there unless transferred elsewhere (Hoffman 1974; Riskin 1975). Because of this direct allocation system, the Chinese do not have to rely on material differentials to attract workers into particular jobs.[2] Another area of greater Chinese control is private life, since more extensive efforts are made to organize after-hours activities for workers, students, and even forced labor camp inmates than is generally the case in the Soviet Union (see Whyte 1974).

We see in post-1949 China, then, a society which has been greatly if not fully bureaucratized. For ordinary citizens much of life is spent in, and interacting with, large-scale, complex organizations which have a hierarchy of ranked offices employing people who have special skills and earn different wage levels. By almost any criterion Weber's 1913 assessment seems fulfilled, if not overfulfilled.

What does the other end of the beast look like, though? Mao set the tone in his 1933 statement, "This great evil, bureaucracy, must be thrown into the cesspool" (Meisner 1971: 29). For Mao and other Chinese Communist leaders, bureaucracy bore the connotation of a venal officialdom which had oppressed the ordinary people for centuries. The intervening years if anything intensified this sentiment. Mao's 1967 statement, "Twenty Manifestations of Bureaucracy," is one of the most forceful indictments ever made on the subject. A few excerpts convey the tone:

> 2. They [bureaucrats] are conceited, complacent, and they aimlessly discuss politics. They do not grasp their work; they are subjective and one-sided; they are careless; they do not listen to the people; they are truculent and arbitrary; they force orders; they do not care about reality; they maintain blind control. This is authoritarian bureaucracy. . . .

> 5. They are ignorant; they are ashamed to ask anything; they exaggerate and they lie; they are very false; they attribute errors to the people; they attribute merit to themselves; they swindle the central government; they deceive those above them and fool those below them; they conceal faults and gloss over wrongs. This is dishonest bureaucracy. . . .

> 16. They fight among themselves for power and money; they extend their hands into the Party; they want fame and fortune; they want positions, and if they do not get it they are not satisfied; they choose to be fat and to be lean; they pay a great deal of attention to wages; they are cosy when it comes to cadres but they care nothing about the masses. This is the bureaucracy that is fighting for power and money. . . .[Joint Publications Research Service 1970: 40-43]

Mao's criticisms covered the range, from the red tape and rigidity familiar to critics of Western bureaucracy, to the corruption and disdain for the common man that have roots as much in China's own bureaucratic tradition.

China's antibureaucratic impulse has been expressed in a variety of ways, and these developed in their fullest form in the years between the Cultural Revolution and Mao's death (1966–76). A number of devices were aimed at checking the arrogance of officials and fostering close ties between them and their subordinates. First, repeated campaigns attacking "bourgeois styles of life" inhibited the development of distinctive patterns of consumption, leisure activities, and so forth among Chinese officials, in spite of their higher pay and power. Bureaucrats also were required to periodically leave their offices for periods of purification through manual labor and political study. For many this occurred in three- to six-month stints spent in rotation on "May 7th cadre schools," farms where cadres grew crops, hauled manure, re-examined their bureaucratic airs, and emulated the lives of nearby peasants. For industrial administrators regular turns at manual labor posts within their firms were required, and commune cadres were required to spend a given number of days each year engaging in ordinary farm labor. In industrial and other kinds of management Stalin's slogan "cadres decide everything" was rejected. Rather, a variety of organiza-tional devices were used to obtain mass inputs in decision making. Usually this took the form of a "three-way alliance" of managers, technical personnel, and ordinary workers sitting on factory revolu-tionary committees and special problem-solving groups. In addition, subordinates were periodically mobilized to write wall posters to expose the arrogance and other faults of their superiors, and the superiors in turn were expected to confess these shortcomings and pledge to do better. All these efforts were justified with an ideology that said that organiza-tional success was to be measured not simply in terms of things like gross output or profits, but in terms of how well bureaucrats conformed to the officially specified "mass line" style of work (see also Whyte 1973).

Many of the devices discussed so far were concerned with fostering an egalitarian spirit within large, hierarchically organized institutions. But there are other aspects of China's antibureaucratic impulse as well. Periodically the Party has mounted mass campaigns designed to upset bureaucratic routines. In a campaign some new goal is proclaimed and all individuals are supposed to be diverted from their normal activities to the pursuit of this goal (whether it be a new kind of work activity, the attack on some group of class enemies, the assault on a health problem, or the inculcation of a new set of popular attitudes). Existing rules and procedures are denounced as hindering mass enthusiasm and initiative, and bureaucrats are pressured to leave their offices and directly lead the masses in campaign activities. Many campaigns have also had a staff simplification component. Existing organizational forms are de-nounced as top-heavy, and bureaucratic staffs are trimmed, with excess personnel "sent down" (xiafang) to jobs at the forefront of production. Another result may be bureaucratic decentralization, with certain organizations and activities removed and placed under the direction of lower-level authorities. Thus some factories, universities, and scientific institutes have been dismantled and relocated in smaller towns and rural areas, in order to be more responsive to local needs. These efforts reflect another of Mao's cryptic directives, "concentrate the large authority, disperse the small authority." In general this means that policy guidance and approved political ideas should be centrally determined, but the details of day-to-day administration should be decentralized where possible to those units best able to judge the problems involved. In general the passion for gigantomania and centralized control characteristic of Soviet organizational life is partly checked in China.

What are we to make of these contradictory bureaucratic and antibureaucratic emphases? Is there, in fact, a beast that meaningfully can combine such contradictory principles? In our view the contradiction is more apparent than real. In some sense China's leaders are so antibureaucratic precisely because the society they have built is so bureaucratic. These leaders clearly recognize the advantages of large-scale organizations in terms of the need to unite and coordinate the activities of the entire population, while keeping promises of material rewards and threats of penal sanctions in the background. The very ambitious nature of the elite's goals requires a very large and complex bureaucratic machine. But such a machine poses three major dangers for the elite. The first is the danger much discussed by Weber and later analysts of bureaucracy. Bureaucratic organizations inevitably develop vested interests and use their claims of special expertise and knowledge to retain their autonomy and resist the efforts of "generalist" political leaders to control them and to induce changes. Parts of the antibureaucratic program in China are designed to prevent this from happening. The "politics in command" ethos stresses that loyalty to the official line determined by the elite has priority over internal organizational performance criteria in judging the behavior of officials. Campaigns and other devices are designed to keep bureaucrats off balance and to prevent them from presenting claims of the form "we know what is best for our organization." For the most part, higher-level control is maintained not through threats of arrest or demotion (although both do occur), but through periodic mobilizations of subordinates to scrutinize and attack the defects of their superiors. The aim is clearly to sandwich administrators in between pressure from higher levels and criticism from below, so that they will remain responsive to the rapidly shifting goals and priorities of a revolutionary society.[3]

The second problem is one of particular concern to socialist theory. It involves the issue of whether socialism can create a classless society, or whether a new system of classes, based not upon property but upon bureaucratic ranks, will inevitably emerge. The well-known analysis of "new class" phenomena presented by Milovan Djilas (1957)[4] is rejected by Soviet ideologists, who see their society divided up into only two major classes (on the one hand workers and employees in state enterprises, including everyone from party leaders to janitors, and on the other hand collective farmers) as well as one "stratum" (the intelligentsia). But at least one segment of the Chinese leadership has recognized the dangers that stratification based upon bureaucratic rank poses for their egalitarian revolution. The ideological explanations used are somewhat contorted, since these leaders are unwilling to abandon completely the property-based conception of class presented in classical Marxism. Thus they tend to talk in terms of "remnants" left over from capitalist society (referred to in a 1975 campaign as "bourgeois right"), and of harmful political attitudes that have their origin in the old exploiting classes and just happen to infect those holding high bureaucratic positions more than most others. But still there is a clear awareness that current position (rather than past property ownership) creates strata in Chinese socialism which exhibit class-like qualities (a sense of common interests, differentiated lifestyles, a different mental outlook, a desire to pass on advantages to one's offspring, etc.).[5] Many of the antibureaucratic devices we have discussed can also be seen, then, as an effort to check the emergence of a bureaucratic "new class."

The third major danger is that bureaucratic hierarchy and privilege will have a negative effect on the enthusiasm and productivity of the ordinary workers and peasants who are the subordinates in Chinese organizations. Chinese development strategy places a major emphasis on mass mobilization, and Chinese leaders feel that eliciting the diligence and enthusiasm of those who labor with their hands is a key factor in economic growth. Many of the recent antibureaucratic devices seem aimed at convincing these laboring masses that they are active participants in their organizations, rather than passive followers of orders from on high.

We have identified three major dangers that help to provoke the antibureaucratic impulse in China: bureaucratic rigidity and vested interests, bureaucratic privilege and inequality, and subordinate dissatisfaction. Concern with these dangers has clearly been modified and reduced since the death of Mao Zedong in 1976 and the subsequent purge of his more radical followers, including his widow. The argument that there is a danger of a "new class" forming among bureaucrats and higher intellectuals is expressly rejected by Mao's successors.[6] Chinese media have been filled in recent years with unfamiliar themes: the need for respect for authority and for rules and regulations, the importance of profits as a success indicator, and the need to provide more latitude and respect for those with technical expertise. In schools, factories, and offices the revolutionary committee form of administration, which included representatives of subordinates within the organization, has been abandoned in favor of a return to rule by directors, chancellors, and similar titled officials. Some decentralized and disbanded institutions have been restored to their previous form, and many "sent down" personnel have been reassigned to specialized work at higher administrative levels. The campaign style of pursuing goals has been criticized as of less-than-universal utility, particularly in the realm of economic production. At the same time, however, there have been new efforts to uncover and criticize abuses of authority by leadership personnel, and new waves of wall posters and letters to newspapers have been encouraged as part of this effort. Arbitrary dictation to local factories and communes by higher authorities also has been sharply criticized, and a variety of forms of required manual labor for leadership personnel still receive stress. Clearly the balance has shifted in important ways, but the post-Mao leadership does not display anything like unqualified admiration for the virtues of bureaucracy.[7]

If the rationale for the dialectical union between bureaucracy and antibureaucracy is clear, does it work well in practice? In other words, have the Chinese managed to create large-scale organizations which successfully avoid the three major problems we have discussed? No general conclusion will be offered here, but we will examine one particular kind of Chinese organization in an attempt to assess the distinctiveness of the Chinese formula. That organization is the people's commune, which we will compare with its Soviet counterpart, the *kolkhoz*.

The average Soviet *kolkhoz* was composed, until around 1950, of about eighty peasant households. An amalgamation campaign begun at that time produced larger units, which now have about four hundred households on the average. Socialization of agriculture in China initially produced agricultural producers' cooperatives roughly comparable in size, but these were subsequently transformed into people's communes which now average perhaps three thousand households. The Chinese organization is thus much larger, but the impression one gets from reading both literatures is that the Soviet form is in some sense more bureaucratic. Let us look at the two institutions and see what differentiates them. Before doing this we may note that they bear many common features. In both, peasants work in collectivized fields under cadre (nonfamilial) leadership and earn work effort units (labor days in the *kolkhoz*, work points in the commune) whose value is dependent upon the size of the final harvest. In each society peasants live in private housing and use the produce of small private plots to enrich their diet and to sell in free peasant markets to supplement their earnings from collectivized labor. Rural party organizations supervise and regulate both organizations.

What are the critical differences then? In the Soviet Union the *kolkhoz* chairman has in most periods been an outsider sent in to direct things and liable to removal at the discretion of higher authorities, rather than by the vote of *kolkhoz* members. Before amalgamation most farms did not even have enough party members to form a primary party organization, and various outside agencies were used to control the farms. Farms did not have their own machinery, but depended upon machine tractor stations (MTS) to provide it. The MTS in fact gave directions about such things as the sown area and the crop mix, and collected the grain to be delivered to the state. Agronomists and other skilled personnel were attached not to individual farms but to the MTS or local agricultural ministry organs. The *raion* (district) party secretary was held directly responsible for the operation of farms within his area, and in particular for the success of state grain procurements there. Although at various times directives were issued warning the *raion* secretary not to interfere in the daily operations of the farms, the severe pressures he was under made him do just that. *Kolkhoz* directors and peasants became familiar with the sudden visits of *raion* officials, which resulted in threats and demands for sudden changes in farm activities. The "outsider" chairman generally saw his primary duty as satisfying the demands of *raion* officials, rather than ensuring proper incentives and enthusiasm among the peasants he was leading. The chairman's pay was based upon a complicated formula including workdays, a fixed salary component, and bonuses for fulfillment of official quotas, particularly in regard to procurements (Hough 1971; Bienstock et al. 1944; Nove 1963, 1967).

After the 1950s amalgamations, several parts of this picture changed. The larger farms generally had primary party organizations, and agencies of external control were less necessary. The MTS disbanded in 1957, with their machinery sold to local farms and their skilled personnel reassigned there and given state pay supplements to maintain their standard of living. The smaller *kolkhozy* of earlier years often became brigades within the larger farms, with certain fields, laborers, machinery, and animals assigned to them. But the farm chairman (still usually an outsider, often reassigned from work in urban areas) was still responsible for the achievement of farm quotas, and he fulfilled these by issuing commands and orders to brigade leaders. Procurement prices were raised, a system of guaranteed minimum pay for collective farmers was introduced, and some shift from state concern with procurements to more stress on agricultural output occurred. But the *raion* authorities were still held responsible for the success of farms in their areas and were pressured for immediate results; the penchant for inspection visits and arbitrary commands continued.

The result of this system of collectivized agriculture has been a fair amount of success in extracting grain procurements to feed the cities and to finance the industrialization drive, but much less success in just about any other indicator of agricultural performance. In particular, the ways in which commands from above have distorted the operation of farms are well known. One student of the subject presents the picture as follows:

> Officials urge the adoption of sowing or harvesting methods, or dates of starting or completion, which look good in the report rather than the most suitable in the given circumstances. To fulfill high delivery targets, farms are ordered to deliver seed grain, or produce required for its own animals and its own peasants. They are told to overslaughter if big meat-delivery plans are required by the center, or they are forbidden to slaughter aged and unproductive cows if the center, alarmed by overslaughtering, has urged the buildup of herds. Crop rotations are repeatedly broken up, corn is ordered to be sown in unsuitable areas, and fallow must be cultivated even if (as in parts of Kazakhstan) it is essential to have more fallow. Obedience to the expressed or implied wishes of the party headquarters, and not efficient farm operations, becomes the dominant determinant of official behavior. [Nove 1963: 66]

These features of *kolkhoz* life have led Western analysts to argue that collectivized agriculture, because of its bureaucratic nature, is inevitably less efficient and less productive than private agriculture. The argument is that farming requires local initiative to respond to varying soil and changing weather conditions, but that the bureaucratic structure of the collective farm prevents this local initiative from operating (see Laird and Laird 1970).

The social consequences of Soviet collectivized agriculture are also clear. Farms are internally stratified, in terms of rewards and power, into managerial personnel, technical personnel, machinery operators, and agricultural laborers. We have noted that Soviet ideology sees the primary class division in the countryside as one between collective farm members and workers on state farms. Soviet sociological research shows, however, that in terms of things like housing patterns, religious beliefs, access to education, and other characteristics, the agricultural laborers on state and collective farms look quite similar, but both look different from the managerial and technical personnel in either kind of farm (see Arutunyan 1966). No doubt the practice of sending in the top farm personnel from the outside rather than promoting them from manual work posts within the farm is a primary reason for this gap. It is clear, then, that new class phenomena are a fact of life in rural Russia today.

The depressing history of collectivized agriculture in the Soviet Union, particularly in the Stalin years, suggests that low peasant work motivation and peasant dissatisfaction have been serious problems as well. However, it is less certain how great a role the bureaucratic form of farm organization plays in this dismal record, and how much can be attributed to other factors, such as the coercive way farms were originally formed, and the pittance peasants received for many years for their labors (see Bauer et al. 1956; Abramov 1963; Amalrik 1970).

When we turn to the case of the Chinese commune, we see a number of important differences that offset initial impressions based upon size alone. At first, in 1958–60, the communes exhibited many of the same problems we have detailed for the Soviet *kolkhoz*, but since then a program of decentralization has altered the picture. The subordinate brigade and team levels have become much more important administratively. The team, composed of twenty to forty households of close kinsmen and lifelong neighbors, has become the basic accounting unit. This means that the team has its own fields, machinery, and personnel, and that remuneration of team members depends on the harvests of the team itself, and not on those of the entire brigade or commune (as in 1958–60). The team has to negotiate its annual production plan with higher levels and may be pressured to adopt a mix of crops different from what team members would prefer.[8] But once the plan is set, the day-to-day decisions about labor allocation and other matters are made by the team cadres, without much interference from higher levels. The brigade and commune are units used to coordinate larger-scale activities—small fertilizer factories, tool workshops, irrigation and land reclamation projects, etc. The latter projects, and even some of the small factories, are run on a seasonal basis rather than full time, so that they do not compete with the labor requirements of team farming. The team and brigade cadres are almost always all local people rather than outsiders, and as such their primary loyalties are to the peasants they lead, rather than to the external bureaucracy. Rather than fixed salaries, they earn work points only marginally higher in value than those of the average peasant they lead, and there is a fair amount of mobility into and out of these positions. Most often replacements occur because a rural cadre is unwilling to put up with the pressures of a job with so little material benefit, rather than because higher-level authorities are dissatisfied with his performance.[9] Some of the skilled personnel in the commune have been paid in similar ways. Workers in brigade factories, barefoot doctors, and machinery operators generally earn work points' whose value depends on the size of the harvest, rather than fixed salaries paid by the commune or state. Since not all these people could be expected to contribute to higher harvests through their efforts, the aim is clearly not one of incentives but of preventing strata based upon differential forms of pay from emerging. Only the distant commune cadres and specialists, some of whom are outsiders, receive fixed salaries and benefits. Commune peasants can look around and see that most of the people directly leading and advising them do not differ from themselves very much in either background or pay.

Chinese policy also emphasizes production increases more than simple procurements, perhaps because Chinese agriculture after 1949 had less of a cushion of extractable surplus than Russian agriculture in 1928. Most of the state budget in China comes from industrial profits rather than from extractions from the countryside. State grain taxes were fixed in the 1950s and have constituted a generally decreasing proportion of the harvest since then.[10] The retained profits from farming activities are for the most part retained locally, with a portion used for investment in rural schools, health care plans, commune industry, and other projects, rather than simply distributed to team members to consume. This accords with the Chinese emphasis on self-reliance, and makes it less necessary to expend state resources on such projects.

In operation Chinese communes seem to work quite differently from their Soviet counterparts. Since the disastrous great leap forward period (1958–60) the record of agricultural growth has been fairly steady, unlike the erratic ups and downs of Soviet agriculture (of course, weather as well as human factors may be responsible[11]). The commune seems to provide an effective structure for undertaking those large-scale projects requiring specialized skills and resources, while still retaining a small unit which can exercise initiative and respond to rapidly changing conditions in day-to-day farming. Higher level directives to invest in new projects or to alter the crop mix do occur, but interference in daily farming operations seems slight.[12] China has carried out her own "green revolution" since the early 1960s, and has begun to grow rice and other crops in areas where they had not been grown before. But this usually seems to have been done without the sorts of irrationality and waste of the Soviet corn campaigns and other activities. One reason is that an effective agricultural extension service has been built in China which makes it possible to combine higher-level direction with peasant participation and experimentation. Communes, brigades, and teams are all urged to run small experimental plots where new seeds and farming techniques can be tried out to see if they are suited to local conditions. The decentralized agricultural research institutes have a large part of their personnel assigned to field stations at all times, working with local peasants to assess the wisdom of introducing new crops and methods. As a result, only those innovations that seem suited to local conditions are generally accepted. Within the commune frequent consultations among peasant experimenters at different levels aid in this assessment (Stavis 1974). Again the flexibility of the commune structure and its ability to combine local initiative with higher-level coordination and direction are visible (see Stavis 1976; Uphoff and Esman 1974; Perkins 1976).[13]

In terms of social consequences the commune also looks different from its Soviet counterpart. The commune cadres and specialists are a different breed from the ordinary peasants in terms of their backgrounds, power, and pay, but these individuals for the most part do not intervene in team activities on a day-to-day basis. Leaders in the team and brigade come from the locality and are not noticeably different, in terms of pay or other characteristics, from those led; a cadre today may be an ordinary peasant tomorrow. The important material differences that exist are those between families with many or few work-point earners, and between peasants in teams with high daily work-point value and low daily work-point values (teams within a single brigade may have pay differentials as great as three or four to one). Thus, at least in terms of the lower ranges of the commune structure, new class phenomena are not very important, while family, team, and village differences remain highly salient. In some ways this sort of economic stratification is not all that different from rural China before 1949, and looks quite different from Chinese state farms, which have a system of set wages determined by position, seniority, and other factors. For Chinese peasants today the scene is not one of individuals attached to particular ranks and wages, but of corporate family units whose fortunes rise and fall as children mature, daughters marry out, and older members die.

The Chinese commune consists, then, of a new administrative structure superimposed fairly effectively on a structure of natural village and family units which are given continued vitality and importance. The great advantage of the structure is its flexibility, with the ability to combine higher direction with local initiative and incentive. But the system has some disadvantages from the official point of view as well. Since the fundamental loyalties of the local cadres lie with fellow villagers rather than with the external bureaucracy, when that bureaucracy wants to institute major changes it may have difficulty doing so. The Chinese elite promotes radical changes in rural family life (elimination of bride prices, simple and secularized wedding ceremonies, sexual equality, etc.), but for the most part peasants can ignore official directives in these matters, secure in the knowledge that local cadres would not want to jeopardize their community standing by cracking down on traditional customs. In 1968–71 the elite tried to institute equalizing reforms in rural life—brigade- rather than team-level management and farming, a more egalitarian work-point system, etc.—but these reforms threatened the interests of the family and team units upon which the commune is based. Confronted with peasant grumbling and poor work performance, these reforms eventually had to be rescinded.[14] In general the decentralization of the structure and the policy of self-reliance make it difficult for the state to redistribute resources so as to improve the standing of poorer families and teams. The current structure clearly has a certain inertia and set of vested interests, making it less responsive to higher controls than it might otherwise be. So China's leaders have produced a form of collectivized agriculture which operates fairly effectively and inhibits the development of new class forces, but, partly as a consequence of that effectiveness, is not as responsive to central command as China's leaders would sometimes like.

We have argued that the bureaucratic and antibureaucratic impulses in China today can be seen as complementary rather than contradictory. They represent attempts to reap the advantages of large-scale organizations while avoiding a number of dangers bureaucracy poses for revolutionary rulers. At least in the sphere of agriculture, these impulses have led to a form of organization which, while larger than its Soviet counterpart, is in important ways less bureaucratic. But even the commune cannot be regarded by China's leaders as a victory over all bureaucratic evils; perhaps we can say that successful bureaucracies everywhere are less responsive to demands for change than unsuccessful ones. And if criticisms aired in the Chinese press since 1976 are any guide, urban factories, schools, and offices have not been characterized by the flexibility and high work motivation built into the commune structure. Examination of the Chinese case suggests that we should be wary of drawing hard and fast conclusions about the inevitable consequences of bureaucratization (or for that matter, of Leninist political institutions). Just as with socialism, there is bureaucracy, and then again there is bureaucracy.

Notes

1. See, for example, Pfeffer 1973. Not all recent observers would agree with Pfeffer's view. For a contrary account, see Leys 1977.

2. Individuals in China can quit their jobs, and some may be able to use their contacts in bureaucratic channels to arrange a job transfer. The difficulty comes mainly in trying to get a new job without going through the proper bureaucratic channels. It should be noted, however, that in urban areas there are some temporary jobs and small-scale cooperative factory posts that are not part of the bureaucratic job allocation system described here.

3. Some students of the subject maintain that the result of this dual pressure situation is the opposite of what is intended; that officials react by becoming more timid and cautious, making it necessary to apply very great pressure to get even modest goals complied with. See Vogel 1971. This latter view is

supported by statements in the Chinese press since Mao's death that the shifting pressures and campaigns instituted by "the gang of four" (Mao's radical supporters in the leadership) had a terrible effect on the initiative and responsiveness of organizational leaders. See, for example, British Broadcasting Corporation 1978.

4. Earlier critiques along similar lines arose within the communist movement. See Luxemburg 1935; Trotsky 1937.

5. The clearest statements of these views were offered in 1975 by members of the ruling Politburo who have since been purged as part of "the gang of four." See Yao 1975; Chang 1975.

6. See *Jen-min Jih-pao*, 8 October 1977; *Red Flag*, no. 11, 1977, pp. 61–64; *Kuang-ming Jih-pao*, 20 February 1978.

7. For representative arguments on these and related themes, see *Jen-min Jih-pao*, 31 October 1977; 7 December 1977; 12 March 1978; 27 May 1978. Also see *Peking Review*, no. 40, 30 September 1977, p. 9; no. 12, 24 March 1978, pp. 15–17.

8. In particular, official policy has often required each locality to sow at least part of its fields in food grains, even if concentrating exclusively on commercial crops would be more profitable. In the period since 1976 this policy has been modified somewhat, though, to encourage more crop specialization.

9. Evidence for these assertions is based on interviews with former residents of villages in Kwangtung province. See Parish and Whyte 1978.

10. In 1978 it was announced, however, that grain taxes had begun to be calculated on the basis of the average yields of the years 1971–75. Peasants are to be at least partly compensated for the increase in these taxes by a raise in the state purchasing price paid for grain procured after the taxes have been collected. See *Peking Review*, no. 52, 29 December 1978, p. 7.

11. Since these lines were originally written some of the luster of the Chinese foodgrain production record has dimmed, as from 1974–77 there was apparently minimal growth rather than the sustained increases of the previous decade. It is uncertain what to attribute this leveling off to—poor weather, shortages in inputs like machinery and chemical fertilizer, or new problems in motivation and outside interference (see below).

12. When a team is felt to be running its production or political affairs very poorly the commune or county authorities may organize a special "work team" to go in and temporarily take command to try to right the situation. But this is a fairly unusual and drastic measure.

13. In the period since 1976 the Chinese press has carried a number of articles denouncing instances in which higher authorities were placing cropping and other demands on localities that did not fit local conditions, thus producing poor results. Press articles also criticize higher-level pressures that led communes to divert too high a proportion of their resources into various investment projects and therefore not enough into peasant consumption, thus undermining work incentives. We are uncertain how typical the cases pointed to in the press are, since our interviews dealing with rural Kwangtung up through 1974 convinced us that such arbitrary interventions in production matters were quite unusual. See Parish and Whyte 1978.

However, the recent difficulties and criticisms lead us to qualify a bit the argument developed in the preceding pages. The structure of the Chinese commune is designed to embody decentralized flexibility. However, its mode of operation is not engraved in stone or protected by legal or similar guarantees, and thus depends on the extent to which higher authorities recognize the virtues of this flexibility and avoid arbitrary pressures and interference. During most of the period since 1961, and in most places, this has been the situation, but there have been some important exceptions.

14. The mixed record of success in implementing rural changes is documented in Parish and Whyte 1978. For systematic discussions of the commune structure and its operations in recent years, see Crook 1975 and Ahn 1975.

References

Abramov, F.
  1963   *The New Life: A Day on a Collective Farm*. New York: Grove Press.
Ahn, B. J.
  1975   The Political Economy of the People's Commune in China: Changes and Continuities. *Journal of Asian Studies* 34 (May): 631–658.
Amalrik, A.
  1970   *Involuntary Journey to Siberia*. New York: Harcourt Brace Jovanovich.
Arutunyan, Yu V.
  1966   The Social Structure of the Rural Population. Translated in *Current Digest of the Soviet Press* 18(25): 20–25.
Bauer, R., A. Inkeles, and C. Kluckhohn
  1956   *How the Soviet System Works*. Cambridge: Harvard University Press.
Bienstock, G., S. Schwarz, and A. Yugow
  1944   *Management in Russian Industry and Agriculture*. London: Oxford University Press.
British Broadcasting Corporation
  1978   *Summary of World Broadcasts: The Far East*. FE/5806/BII/9-14, May 6. London.
Chang, Ch'un-ch'iao
  1975   On Exercising All-round Dictatorship over the Bourgeoisie. *Peking Review*, 4 April.
Crook, Frederick W.
  1975   The Commune System in the People's Republic of China, 1963-1974. In Joint Economic Committee, Congress of the United States, *China: A Reassessment of the Economy*. Washington, D.C.: U.S. Government Printing Office.
Djilas, Milovan
  1957   *The New Class*. New York: Praeger.
Funnell, Victor C.
  1971   Bureaucracy and the Chinese Communist Party. *Current Scene* 5: 6.
Hoffman, Charles
  1974   *The Chinese Worker*. Albany, N.Y.: SUNY Press.

Hough, Jerry F.
  1971   The Changing Nature of the Kolkhoz Chairman. In James R. Millar
          (ed.), *The Soviet Rural Community*. Urbana: University of Illinois
          Press.
Joint Economic Committee, Congress of the United States
  1975   *China: A Reassessment of the Economy*. Washington, D.C.: U.S.
          Government Printing Office.
Joint Publications Research Service
  1970   Chairman Mao Discusses Twenty Manifestations of Bureaucracy.
          Translations on Communist China 90: 40–43.
Kao, Ying-mao
  1971   Patterns of Recruitment and Mobility of Urban Cadres. In John W.
          Lewis (ed.), *The City in Communist China*. Stanford: Stanford
          University Press.
Karcz, Jerzy (ed.)
  1967   *Soviet and East European Agriculture*. Berkeley: University of
          California Press.
Laird, Roy D. (ed.)
  1963   *Soviet Agricultural and Peasant Affairs*. Lawrence: University of
          Kansas Press.
Laird, Roy D., and Betty A. Laird
  1970   *Soviet Communism and Agrarian Revolution*. Baltimore: Penguin.
Leys, Simon
  1977   *Chinese Shadows*. New York: Viking.
Luxemburg, Rosa
  1935   *Leninism or Marxism?* Glasgow: Anti-Parliamentary Communist
          Federation.
Meisner, Maurice
  1971   Leninism and Maoism: Some Populist Perspectives on Marxism-
          Leninism in China. *China Quarterly* 45: 29.
Nove, Alec
  1963   Incentives for Peasants and Administrators. In Roy D. Laird (ed.),
          Soviet Agricultural and Peasant Affairs. Lawrence: University of
          Kansas Press.
  1967   Peasants and Officials. In Jerzy Karcz (ed.), *Soviet and East European
          Agriculture*. Berkeley: University of California Press.
Parish, William L., and Martin King Whyte
  1978   *Village and Family in Contemporary China*. Chicago: University of
          Chicago Press.
Perkins, Dwight
  1976   A Conference on Agriculture. *China Quarterly* 67: 596–610.
Pfeffer, Richard M.
  1973   Leaders and Masses. In Michel Oksenberg (ed.), *China's Develop-
          mental Experience*. New York: Praeger.
Riskin, Carl
  1975   Workers' Incentives in Chinese Industry. In Joint Economic Com-
          mittee, Congress of the United States, *China: A Reassessment of the
          Economy*. Washington, D.C.: U.S. Government Printing Office.
Schurmann, Franz
  1968   *Ideology and Organization in Communist China*. 2nd ed. Berkeley:
          University of California Press.

Stavis, Benedict
    1974   *Making Green Revolution: The Politics of Agricultural Develop-
            ment in China.* Ithaca, N.Y.: Cornell University Rural Development
            Committee.
    1976   China's Rural Local Institutions in Comparative Perspective. *Asian
            Survey* 16: 381–96.
Trotsky, Leon
    1937   *The Revolution Betrayed.* Garden City, N.Y.: Doubleday.
Uphoff, Norman T., and Milton J. Esman
    1974   *Local Organization for Rural Development: Analysis of the Asian
            Experience.* Ithaca, N.Y.: Cornell University Rural Development
            Committee.
Vogel, Ezra F.
    1971   Politicized Bureaucracy: Communist China. *Newsletter on Com-
            parative Studies of Communism* 13: 23–33.
Weber, Max
    1968   *Economy and Society.* New York: Bedminster.
Whyte, Martin King
    1973   Bureaucracy and Modernization in China: The Maoist Critique.
            American Sociological Review 38(2): 149–63.
    1974   *Small Groups and Political Rituals in China.* Berkeley: University of
            California Press.
Yao, Wen-yuan
    1975   On the Social Basis of the Lin Piao Anti-Party Clique. *Peking
            Review*, 7 March.

9.

Incipient Bureaucracy: The Development of Hierarchies in Egalitarian Organizations

KATHERINE NEWMAN

One of the enduring themes in the literature on bureaucracy involves the question of whether or not bureaucracy is destined to become the dominant form of social organization in modern society. Max Weber, acknowledged by many as the father of modern sociology, certainly seemed to believe this was the case. In Weber's view, the movement of history was to be understood as the progressive development of rationalization, a trend most clearly reflected in the growth and pervasiveness of bureaucracy as an organizational form.

Weber was convinced that bureaucratic rationality represented a step forward in the administration of human society. He saw bureaucracy as technically superior to those forms of social organization which had prevailed during earlier historical periods. Among the more significant features of bureaucracy, Weber identified the following:

1. There is the principle of fixed and official jurisdictional areas, which are generally ordered by rules. . . .
2. The principles of office hierarchy and of levels of graded authority mean a firmly ordered system of super- and subordination in which there is supervision of the lower offices by the higher ones. . . .
3. The management of the modern office is based upon written documents. . . .
4. Office management, at least all specialized office management . . . usually presupposes thorough and expert training. . . .
5. When the office is fully developed, official activity demands the full working capacity of the official. . . .
6. The management of the office follows general rules, which are more or

less stable, more or less exhaustive, and which can be learned. [Weber 1947, quoted in Grusky and Miller 1970: 5]

Thus, in contrast to "patrimonial" forms of administration, bureaucracy encouraged and indeed required that predictable, dependable methods of goal attainment be instituted. Rational rules replaced the whims of ad hoc decision makers; qualifications for positions developed where entirely ascriptive characteristics had previously prevailed; circumscribed, hierarchically distributed responsibilities took the place of kin-based or personalistic obligations; in short, rationalization as a "master trend" in history was manifested in the increasing accountability which bureaucratic organizations reflected.

While Weber was enormously impressed by the efficiency and technological superiority of bureaucracies, his intellectual descendants were not completely convinced. Two traditions within the sociology of formal organizations have turned a critical eye on this assumption. Some individuals have looked at the inefficiencies of bureaucratic organizations and attempted to identify the systematic sources of these problems. A second tradition has searched for alternative forms of organization which might conceivably prove superior to bureaucracy. These scholars have examined various types of institutions which are formally committed to egalitarianism in the belief that they constitute the most fertile soil for the growth of nonbureaucratic forms of organization. They have then attempted to delineate both the pressures which lead toward bureaucratization, and conversely, those which tend to retard hierarchy formation in organizations oriented toward egalitarianism. Thus, for example, Robert Michels (1959) studied oligarchy formation in egalitarian political parties; Lipset, Trow, and Coleman (1956) examined the sociological bases of democracy in trade unions; and Rae Blumberg (1976) investigated the nature of social equality and emergent sexual stratification in socialist Israeli *kibbutzim*.

The present study follows in this latter tradition. We will be investigating one particular kind of organization, the workers' collective, in an attempt to pinpoint the forces which both promote and retard the development of bureaucratization within the organization. We will pay special attention to the relationship between the egalitarian collectives and the hierarchical bureaucracies with which they had to coexist in the wider sociocultural environment. Our concern is to determine whether or not "alternative" organizations such as the workers' collectives can compete with bureaucratic institutions without losing their distinctive, nonstratified characteristics.

The data for this paper were drawn from ethnographic histories of twelve organizations located in urban areas of northern and southern

California. Like the institutions studied by the sociologists mentioned above, the workers' collectives were overtly committed to antibureaucratic, egalitarian forms of organization. As such, they exhibited the reverse of Weber's description of a formal bureaucracy: there was no system of "graded authority," very little in the way of "expert training," a rather fluid attitude toward rules, and a minimum number of written documents of the sort Weber had in mind. On the contrary, the collectives placed a high value on preserving an egalitarian, consensus-based process of decision making. They downplayed or eliminated the need for specialized training. They eschewed the need for abstract rules, preferring to depend on face-to-face communication as the major medium of conducting "business." In short, the collectives made a point of rejecting the Weberian dictum that bureaucracy was the most efficient and rational form of administration, opting instead for organizational features which were at odds with the "ideal type" notion of bureaucracy and were instead intended to maintain egalitarianism.

As we shall see below, some of the collectives included in this study *were* able to create and sustain the ideal organization they had hoped for. However, most of them moved toward hierarchical structures of authority, thus metamorphosing into the opposite of what they had intended to be. In the sections which follow we will attempt to explain how "incipient bureaucracies" developed within the collectives and to delineate those forces which contributed to the erosion of egalitarianism and the development of bureaucracy.

The Cultural Milieu of the Collectives

The late 1960s provided a cultural forum for experimentation in the United States. Individuals left the city for rural communes, rock concerts were transformed from purely musical events into expressions of community and cooperation (e.g., the Woodstock "nation"), and freedom from institutional restraints became the goal of young people throughout the country. Among the primary themes of this period, there were two that should be understood as background to the founding of the workers' collectives we are concerned with: (1) alternative ways of life were considered to be pragmatically possible, rather than merely desirable; and (2) collective activities were considered preferable to individualistic ones, since they fostered a harmonious spirit rather than competitive hostility. These values were widespread during the antiwar era and they constituted the foundation upon which a number of institutional innovations were built (Berger 1971).

The people who formed workers' collectives during this period were often "refugees" from the bureaucratic worlds of business, of college, and of government-sponsored social service. What the so-called "countercultural" milieu meant to them was an opportunity to engage in meaningful work, free from the trappings of time cards, bosses, rule books, and formal attire. In short, it was bureaucracy (among other things) that they wanted to leave behind. They wanted to demonstrate that successful organizations could be built on principles of equality and cooperation, rather than of hierarchy and coercion. It was not enough to embrace these as ideals; one had to demonstrate that they were *viable alternatives,* ones which could be actualized, for it was only upon demonstrating viability that nonbureaucratic institutions could be shown to be superior to their "straight" counterparts.

It was against this profoundly antibureaucratic, proegalitarian backdrop that the urban workers' collectives were constructed. By their own definition, they were organizations which practiced communal decision making by allocating equal authority to every member. No individual was to be considered more important than any other, and all actions had to be agreed upon by the entire body. The division of labor within the collectives was often fixed, but individuals were rotated through the variety of positions available so that no one became "stuck" in one spot as people did in traditional bureaucratic institutions.

A Typology of Collectives

The structural features mentioned above, namely egalitarian authority distribution and rotating division of labor, were structural features common to the twelve collectives included in this study. However, there were differences between them as well, some of which became significant in explaining why some were more successful than others in resisting bureaucratization. These differences prompt us to consider three different types of collectives.

The "business collectives" were those which either produced a product for competitive sale or offered retail products and services to the public. Typical of the business collectives were health food stores, leather shops, and printing operations. Like all businesses, these collectives depended upon commercial trade for their income and were in competition with noncollectivized, hierarchically organized businesses. The important feature shared by these business collectives was the selling of a product to the public or to other businesses. Within the sample of twelve organizations included in this study, three of them were business collectives by this definition.

The second type of organization was the "service collective." These organizations were also involved with the public and, as their name indicates, they offered services. Here we find alternative schools, child care centers, legal advisory collectives, and the like. The crucial difference between the business and service collectives is that while the former received some kind of payment from the consumer, the latter did not. The service collectives did not, on the whole, depend on consumers for financial support. Among the collectives examined in this study, the four "service collectives" were free to their clients, although one accepted voluntary donations.

"Information collectives" formed the third group and were markedly different from the other two in that they did not provide any consumable goods or services to the public. What they did have to offer was a source of information on topics ranging from rape prevention to employment to nutrition and mental health. Some of these organizations aimed at narrow special interests and some were very broadly conceived to appeal to anyone with a concern for the topic in question. The most typical information collectives were countercultural or political newspapers and hot lines. The remaining five organizations in our sample were of this general type.

We will now go on to examine the "life cycle" of these kinds of organizations. We shall see that at a crucial point many of them had to turn to outside sources of funding in order to remain afloat. The differences between the three types led to differences in the degree to which they ultimately became dependent upon these outside agencies. Part of our argument regarding bureaucratization in the collectives is based upon the nature of the funding sources and the extent to which such assistance was required.

The Life Cycle of the Workers' Collectives

Ethnographic histories of the twelve collectives in the study reveal that at the outset they did closely approximate their idealized view of an egalitarian distribution of authority. There were no formal leaders, nor were there any followers. Each collective member had an equal vote in decisions affecting the operation of each organization. The institutional features which supported such a power distribution generally consisted of frequent group meetings, rotating responsibilities, and extensive informal contact between collective members.

The overt purpose of the group meetings was essentially to allocate individual responsibilities, determine policy regarding the major activities of the organization, and raise questions occasioned by the daily work load. When these collectives were originally founded, these overt purposes were, in fact, the actual accomplishments of the group meetings. We will see that later on in the "life cycle" of the collective, these meetings took on additional significance. However, during the initial stage of development, group meetings did serve as a forum for collective decision making. Although they worked well as far as the implementation of egalitarian ideals were concerned, the meetings were rather time consuming. They occurred on an average of three or four times per week. This time commitment was added to that which was required for the normal nonadministrative activities of each collective: seeing clients, writing newspaper stories, selling food, etc.

At this point, it should be noted that nearly all of the original collective members served as volunteer workers. That is, the activities of the collectives generally constituted a second "job" for most of the participants. Since they were not paid for the work they contributed to the organization, most individuals were holding down paying jobs elsewhere in order to provide for their financial needs. Had they been donating time to orthodox bureaucratic organizations, this might not have proved to be such a burden, since the weight of decision making is rarely felt by volunteers in standard institutions. In the collectives, however, preservation of an egalitarian orientation required that more time-consuming structural features be instituted. This guaranteed that decisions affecting the collective would indeed be made by all the members.

What were the consequences of these double commitments, one to the collective and one to a "straight" job? As the collectives became more and more involved in the business, service, and information areas they were founded for, the pressure to increase the amount of time devoted to collective activities grew. It became increasingly more difficult for members to hold down regular jobs and fulfill their obligations to the collectives. Moreover, since most of the people who belonged to workers' collectives saw these organizations as their primary interest (and their "regular" jobs as necessary evils), they began to search for some way out of the growing time pressure.

The only solution to the problem was to find some source of funding so that collective members could rely upon the collective organizations themselves for their financial needs, thus freeing them from the necessity of holding down two positions simultaneously. The question was, where could such funding sources be found?

For two of the collectives concerned this dilemma was easily solved. The members of the organization were able to invest their own capital in order to provide for operating expenses and minimally adequate salaries. Both of these were what we have termed "business collectives." The fact that they were able to generate enough cash from their own pockets to stay in business was significant. This was possible mainly because the business itself, if successful, would eventually pay its own way. The cash intake from either wholesale or retail trade provided enough to keep these two collectives going strong once they had a sufficient amount of start-up capital.

The "bureaucratization" story ends here for these two collectives, for they never did develop any form of organization other than the egalitarian collectivity they began with. They both continue (to this day) to hold regular group meetings in order to determine business policy and air grievances, and the division of labor is rotated on a frequent basis. In short, these two collectives have been able to retain their original egalitarian format while expanding their membership and enlarging the scope of their businesses.

For the other ten collectives, however, the process of bureaucratization began at the point where they had to solicit outside support. Unable to provide funds from amongst their own membership, they turned to a variety of external agencies for the monies necessary to create collectives staffed by full-time members. The type of financial aid available to the collectives varied somewhat, as shown by our typology. Business collectives could apply to banking institutions for loan funds, while service and information collectives could not. Banks require that organizations demonstrate an ability to repay loans, something which the latter two types of collectives were by definition unable to do. Service and information collectives tended to solicit grants from community agencies, such as federal/local revenue sharing funds dispersed by county boards of supervisors, and from private foundations.

In all cases, these collectives had to convince outsiders that they warranted financial assistance. Those who approached public officials for funds were under pressure to demonstrate that they performed a service which was in demand. Their case was often strengthened if they could argue that they answered the needs of some highly visible minority group (single parents, handicapped people, ethnic minorities, etc.). Since collective members made very modest salary requests, they effectively presented local government agencies with inexpensive ways of satisfying the requests of political pressure groups. In contrast, those who approached the banks were faced with the task of demonstrating their fiscal responsibility and steady income. Obtaining financial assistance from lending institutions posed a different set of problems from those encountered in the pursuit of government monies. Nevertheless, in both situations the collectives were under pressure to persuade standard, highly bureaucratized institutions of their viability.

Success in the world of grants and loans did not come easily to the collectives. Many of them were turned down the first and second times.

One of the most compelling reasons for their initial failure was the fact that the organizational format of the collectives was simply unacceptable to the tradition-bound agencies to which they had applied for help. Collectives, which by definition were without presidents, vice-presidents, treasurers, and the like, were alien to the bureaucratic machinery to which they had turned. Banks were unwilling to take twenty cosigners on a loan form, and county supervisors were not about to turn over federal grant monies to organizations without formal hierarchies. After all, who was to be held responsible for the use of funds? In general, those collectives which sought external assistance discovered that they would have to play by the rules of these large bureaucratic agencies in order to obtain what they needed to stay alive.

This confrontation with the "outside" world was a rather traumatic experience for most of the collectives. For although the central purpose of each organization was to conduct a particular activity—e.g., child care or newspaper publishing—their egalitarian format was in many respects a commitment of equal importance. To capitulate to the bureaucratic requirements of the "straight" world, for the sake of financing distributed by politically dubious sources, was a fate they found exceedingly difficult to accept. However, the membership had little choice in view of the increasing strain of dual time commitments, one to regular jobs and one to the collectives. Furthermore, the prospect of operating the various collectives on more than a bare bones budget had a certain appeal. Services could be expanded, permanent quarters could be rented, and more clients could be handled. Beyond these material advantages, the collectives would have the additional advantage of being "legitimized" in the eyes of the non-countercultural elements of the community at large. The financial support of local government agencies could add a dose of prestige and status which most nontraditional (and politically left) organizations found hard to come by on their own. In the case of the information collectives, many of which were attempting to persuade individuals to take political stands on some issue, this was especially appealing. Thus, for example, in one collective the membership split down the middle on the issue of whether affiliation with government funding agencies would draw them away from their original purpose:

> Debates on financial allotment of money and ideological priorities of the group reconvened. Many members encouraged the group to commit itself to more "grass-roots" activities, specifically the crisis line, speak-outs, and community organizing type functions. Others felt the collective could become an example for other groups, and that its workable relationship with institutions (e.g., the police and the county administration) was the beginning of the collective's credibility and power to begin to legislate institutional changes. [Chao 1977: 10]

Arguments over the pros and cons of associating with politically "tainted" sources of funds continued, even after most of the collectives in this study accepted such resources. Of course, some individuals openly rejected the connotations of "straight" support, preferring instead to maintain their independence and a somewhat "shabby, but free" image among their constituency. For the most part, however, members who took this position left the organization in due course.

How did these organizations solve the double-bind dilemma they found themselves in? How were they able to accept support from the bureaucratic world and yet convince themselves and their clientele that they were not in the process of being coopted? This was not easy. The collectives included in this study tended to solve the problem by capitulating to the demands of funding agencies "in name only." Presidents, vice-presidents, and treasurers were appointed and these individuals put their signatures to the grant proposals and loan forms. They thereby became responsible (in the legal sense) for funds allocated to the collectives. However, it was understood by all inside the organizations that these positions were "phony," created to satisfy the requirements of county supervisors or loan officers, but having no real authority within the collectives themselves.

The structural mechanisms created for the purposes of sustaining egalitarian modes of decision making continued to function as they had before. The ideology of equality continued to dominate within the collectives, thus casting aside whatever implications the "fake" positions might have had for the authority structure of the organizations. In short, people behaved as though the intrusion of outside agencies into their internal affairs was a "non-problem" and concentrated instead on what their new-found riches enabled them to do for the various causes with which they were associated.

However, two factors intervened in this idyllic situation which had the ultimate effect of breathing life into the "name only" bureaucracies. We will examine these factors closely, for it was here that the egalitarian nature of the collectives began to crumble. First of all, the now-salaried collective members became completely dependent upon the resources of the organization for their personal financial needs, having given up their other commitments in favor of full-time paid work for the collectives. This had the effect of increasing their concern for securing funds for the future. Secondly, because the budgets awarded by granting agencies tended to be only minimally sufficient, the collectives had to recruit additional volunteer members in order to deliver what they had promised in their grant packages. Operating together, these two problems began to wreak havoc with the collective form of organization and led to the formation of hierarchies which eventually became entrenched.[1]

Most city/county grant funds are awarded on a yearly basis. This "soft money" situation had the effect of forcing the collectives to devote an ever-increasing amount of time and energy to the solicitation of funds for the next fiscal year. When collective members participated exclusively on a volunteer basis, the time they spent working for the collectives was devoted to the overt tasks of the organization (providing legal advice, producing newsletters, etc.). However, given their newfound dependence on outside money sources for financial sustenance, they had little choice but to play the "grantsmanship game" in a continuous search for financial support. One collective reported that it had to devote roughly two-thirds of its manpower resources to securing grants. Another collective became so expert in the grant business that it took on the task of reviewing grant proposals for other countercultural organizations, giving free advice on strategy.

What did the grantsmanship game entail on the part of the collectives? Primarily, the collectives had to convince community funding agencies that they spoke to some particular demand within the community. The more vocal the constituency of a particular collective, the more likely it was that funding requests would be granted. This involved fairly complicated politicking at open hearings where county supervisors would hear requests for funds. The press was always present at these yearly hearings, since it was here that the voices of political pressure groups could be heard loud and clear. The atmosphere of these open meetings was tense and competitive. The collectives had to marshal their supporters in order to appear to be a rather substantial political force. Of course this proved much easier for those organizations associated with high-profile popular movements. When issues regarding women's problems (employment, child care, job training in nontraditional occupations, etc.) commanded popular attention, collectives which spoke to those issues had an easier time of it. Conversely, if public attention shifted away from these issues, the collectives faced an uphill battle. This was a rather volatile atmosphere, which exacerbated the tension accompanying the yearly forage for support. Not only were collectives pitted against each other in competition for pieces of a limited pie, they also had to compete with bureaucratic organizations which were generally quite adept at the money hunt. The politics of the situation occasionally led to a rather irrational outcome—organizations would be given start-up funds and would then be denied their financial lifelines in the funding rounds of the following year. This happened to a number of collectives, though none of them was included in our sample. Nevertheless, the collectives which were part of the present study were mindful of this possibility, if not anxious about it.

In order to make a convincing case for the demand for their services, the collectives found it necessary to turn to a typical bureaucratic device for substantiation. Internal records of case loads, newspaper subscriptions, and volume of referrals, as well as other "accountability documents," surfaced as evidence of community needs. Although the original purpose of these records was to provide funding sources with information for financial audits, in the context of the scramble for support they took on an important secondary function. They served as proof that the collectives were *successful;* goals were thus defined in very bureaucratic terms, i.e., number of clients served. Slowly but surely the pressure of competing for funds led the collectives to adopt the hallmarks of bureaucracy: they adopted bureaucratic methods of internal accounting; they utilized bureaucratic standards of evaluation; they devoted precious manpower resources to the maintenance of typically bureaucratic fronts for public consumption. Again, they had little choice but to do so. They had to learn the language of the powerful organizations which controlled the purse strings. They had to compete against noncollective, nonegalitarian pressure groups which were formally bureaucratized and very efficient at the use of accountability documents for the purposes of budgetary persuasion.

Having examined the experience of the collectives vis-à-vis external forces, it now behooves us to consider what happened to them on the inside. The first thing to note is that the grant monies obtained through local agencies were distributed in as egalitarian a fashion as possible. One did not find directors with fat salaries, as is often the case in bureaucratized nonprofit organizations. On the contrary, the collectives studied followed a policy of dividing the money into as many salaried positions as possible. For the most part this led to very low, subsistence-level salaries, e.g., $325 per month for a full-time person. The salary distribution was also nonstratified. Paid full-time staff members generally received equal pay.

However, the need to set the pay level at this subsistence point presented a barrier to the policy of equality among members. Since the point of obtaining money for salaries was to free collective workers from the necessity of working in another organization to earn a living wage, it was not possible to lower salaries beyond a certain level. Splitting the total wage bill of a single collective into, for example, twenty-five equal stipends of $50 per month would not provide enough for any individual to live on, and hence would not free any members from the constraints of dual obligations. Thus, in practice the money available to the collectives (which was never as much as they wanted) was split up equally into as many salaries as possible at (or slightly above) the subsistence level.

However, various pressures acted upon the collectives to expand beyond this number of participants. The collectives had often made rather generous promises to granting agencies in their attempts to obtain support. Indeed local government finance pushed collectives into such a "bidding" situation. Consequently, there was more work to be done than could be accomplished by the salaried staff alone. A second pressure came from within the collectives themselves; many of them felt that a strong need for their services existed in the community, and wanted to grow to meet this need. Finally, the level of funding was sometimes so low that there were insufficient funds for all participants already in the collective to be paid to work full time. Therefore, some members quit their outside jobs to join the collectives on a full-time basis, while others remained unpaid volunteers and continued to hold down external employment as well.

In any event, whether to fulfill promises made or for other reasons, the collectives were faced with the prospect of recruiting part-time volunteer labor to supplement the full-time staff. The political sympathies of the collectives and the special interest groups toward which they directed their attention led to the creation of a willing pool of volunteer labor.

Structural differences between these volunteers and the full-time staff emerged very gradually, but eventually succeeded in undermining the egalitarian process of decision making that had obtained prior to the development of external financial dependencies. Serious conflicts developed between the prevailing ideological commitment to egalitarianism and the actual practice of decision making that was beginning to emerge at this stage in the "life cycle" of the collectives. In order to understand how this process of deterioration developed, we must consider in some detail the emergent stratification between the volunteers and the salaried members of these organizations.

The full-time members had a number of structural advantages over the part-time volunteers that contributed to the development of an internal hierarchy that was more than in "name only." For the first time in the history of the collectives, some individuals controlled more information about the daily activities of the organization than others. The paid staff, present on a daily basis, were better informed about the activities of the collective than the volunteer members could possibly be. The literature in the sociology of formal organizations tells us that control over information translates into concentrations of power in social institutions (Gouldner 1954; Collins 1976). Such became the case within the collectives. The full-time members of the collectives were able to exert influence beyond their number, simply because they spoke with authority based upon constant (rather than intermittent) contact with the organization and its day-to-day activities. Decisions which would have previously been delayed until group meetings could be arranged started to be made on the spot by the paid staff, who were, after all, more in touch with immediate situations. Furthermore, the full-time staff was rapidly becoming more specialized in certain phases of organizational management. Given the fluctuating presence of the volunteers, it became somewhat difficult to spread the developing expertise around equally. These differences were exacerbated by the fact that the salaried staff were recruited from the original membership of the collectives. "New" participants had to enter on an entirely different basis. Thus the "salaried" versus "volunteer" dichotomy paralleled an "old" versus "new" distinction.

A further structural difference between these two groups concerned the positions they now found themselves in. The new members were now doing essentially the same thing the full-time staff had once done. That is, the volunteers were attempting to hold down full-time occupations elsewhere in order to take care of personal financial concerns, while at the same time fulfilling a commitment to the collective. From the volunteers' ideological viewpoint, commitment to the collectives took on a higher priority than did their paid jobs; nevertheless, they had to eat, and they were not salaried by their respective collectives.

How did these structural differences between the salaried full-time members and the nonsalaried part-time volunteers affect the decision-making process? Here we must examine the conflicts which developed between the ideology of egalitarianism and the actual procedure by which decisions came to be made.

Decision Making in the Collectives: Ideology and Practice

Because the ideology of egalitarianism persisted as a fundamental rallying point for all of the organizations in this study, the structural mechanisms designed to ensure equal control were retained throughout the life cycle of the collectives. However, the utilization of these structural features (i.e., group meetings) changed very subtly as the objective differences in position between the two groups of members grew.

In theory, group meetings were designed to allow all members of a collective a chance to voice opinions on even the most minute details of ongoing business. Yet precisely those distinctions discussed in the previous section, namely information control and membership status, prevented this from actually taking place. The volunteers had less access to information, which made it difficult for them to speak with authority equal to that of the regular staff. The fact that they were present much less of the time effectively minimized the importance of their contributions to decision-making forums. Of course, this happened over a period of time, as the cumulative differences in time investment became more manifest.

The breakdown in effectiveness of the group meetings began in some organizations when the regular staff began to monopolize the speaking floor. In others, the problem began when full-time members started holding informal meetings in anticipation of meetings of the full membership. Even here, the process was informal and did not constitute (in the beginning) a deliberate attempt to exclude volunteers from having a voice in the affairs of the organization. Rather, the convenience of having the most knowledgeable members in the same place on a daily basis led to informal conversations about organizational policy. Nevertheless, this casual procedure happened with considerable regularity. Consequently, the regular staff often entered the general forum with a prearranged policy to recommend. This did not sit well with the volunteer membership, since they rightfully felt excluded from an important part of the decision-making process.

Thus, for example, in one collective devoted to problems affecting women in a southern California community, the membership began to feel as though they were being deliberately shut out of debates over organizational policy:

> About a month after we'd started [the newest program of services within the collective], [volunteer] women expressed increasing dissatisfaction with the decision-making process; we felt powerless. The business meetings allegedly involved us all equally in decision-making, but in actuality [the paid staff] made decisions and informed us of them. [Powell 1977: 7]

Conflicts such as this were reported by many of the collectives in this study. However, these sorts of problems were exceedingly difficult to raise in an explicit fashion, despite the fact that the workers' collectives maintained a self-image of openness, and an aura of almost "encounter group" honesty.

There were two reasons why difficulties regarding the "real" (as opposed to the "ideal") process of decision making were left unarticulated. First of all, a great deal of emotional effort went into the development and maintenance of the ideology of communalism. To admit that the organization was experiencing difficulty in actualizing its political/organizational ideals was tantamount to declaring that the pragmatic goals of equality and nonstratified authority might not be so pragmatic after all. In the midst of external suspicion about the viability of collective organizations, members were loath to admit (openly, at least) that there was something wrong.

The second reason for leaving organizational conflict unspoken concerns the rather vulnerable position of the volunteers within the organizations. The structural position of the volunteers was analogous to the situation of the full-time staff prior to the location of external funding. Yet there was one important difference. By this time, there were salaried positions within the organizations. The existence of these positions made it possible, on occasion, for part-time individuals to move up in the organization when full-time positions were vacated, or when new grant monies were obtained. In short, there were possibilities for upward mobility in organizations that were slowly but surely experiencing the growth of status distinctions between members.

This fact added a further strain to the decision-making process, since group meetings began to take on a secondary function—providing an arena for overt demonstrations of one's suitability for upward movement. To utilize one of Goffman's metaphors, the volunteers were engaged in "presenting a self"; and the elements of that self were loyalty, obvious political commitment, willingness to contribute very long hours on a purely voluntary basis, and an intense interest in every and any problem confronting the collective (Goffman 1959). It was not enough to act upon these commitments; one had to "dramatize" them. Volunteers who wished to distinguish themselves as worthy of consideration for full-time status had to convey a certain self-image, one which was fundamentally congruent with the expectations of those who would *de facto* make hiring decisions. The criteria for success were, of course, never clearly articulated. Individuals were simply aware that some nebulous qualities were required for advancement within the organization. Obviously such an opportunity was available to a very small proportion of the total membership. This served to intensify the "dramaturgical" elements of collective meetings and put additional pressure on individuals not to object to policies which seemed to have the approval of the bureaucratic elite. The lack of explicit criteria for upward mobility exacerbated the situation, giving the full-time staff a clear upper hand in controlling the decision-making process. Thus, for example, a volunteer in one collective commented that:

> Not only are meetings of the [paid staff] closed, but there are no explicit means to becoming a member of this body. We are told that it happens "organically" when we have become "feminist" enough and are willing to commit our lives to the feminist movement and the collective.

What consequences befell an individual who ventured forward with complaints about the decision-making process? Those who did so generally found that they would be subjected to critiques by the regular staff. These criticisms took on a very particular flavor, however. Rather than addressing the existence and growth of a stratified hierarchy within the organization, the "elites" tended to turn the criticism around by inpugning the motives or the political purity of the critic. Instead of meeting the objections regarding the decision-making process, the staff members suggested that the objections were motivated by insufficient commitment to the political goals or substantive tasks confronting the collective. This ideological twist made it virtually impossible for individuals to address the bureaucratization of the collectives openly.

In short, volunteers found themselves unable to express dissenting opinions for fear of quashing their chances to move into the higher ranks. At the same time, the unofficial elite (who would deny that they actually constituted a separate group) had little choice but to maintain the original format of collectivism, despite the fact that egalitarian methods of decision making no longer really prevailed. The conflict between the ideal and the real intensified to the point where in some cases individuals quit and the collective organizations collapsed. In other cases the organizations continued to labor under the pressure of ideological egalitarianism and structural bureaucratization. In the next section we will examine the reasons why some organizations collapsed under the weight of these problems and others did not.

Survival or Extinction

Countercultural organizations such as these collectives were not well known for their staying power. In fact, collectives were often regarded as short-lived phenomena of the late 1960s. There is an element of truth to this view, though the lack of financial support for these organizations may have been more instrumental in their ultimate demise than was lack of interest or effort. Nevertheless, the high casualty rate among workers' collectives is indicative of the difficulties they had in maintaining the alternative organizational format they set out to create.

Of course, not all urban collectives came to an end. Of the organizations included in this study, several of them had been in existence for over five years, despite conflicts of the sort mentioned earlier. What made the difference between those that survived and those that collapsed? In reviewing the ethnographic histories upon which this paper is based, as well as additional materials about the experiences of other collectives, it became clear that one outstanding feature distinguished the "successes" from the "failures": the degree to which the collectives could demonstrate the likelihood that volunteers could actually move up into full-time status.

Collectives which appeared to be totally bottlenecked at the top of the informal hierarchy seemed to stand the least chance of withstanding organizational conflicts. If entrance into the status level of paid, full-time staff member appeared to be out of the question, the organizations simply seemed to fall apart.

On the other hand, collectives which could demonstrate prospects for volunteer mobility in the near future seemed better able to withstand the strain of increasing internal stratification. Either the next round of grant funding promised to make new positions available, or temporary federal funds had been applied for,[2] or the present budget could be manipulated to make room for newcomers somehow. In short, volunteers in this kind of collective could see their way clear to full-time status at some time. This did not put an end to organizational conflict. What it did allow for, however, was the possibility that thoroughly disillusioned members could quit, while the organization as a whole continued on.

Two points should be made about this latter type of collective. One is simply that the need to "toe the party line" was exacerbated beyond what it had been at any other point in the life cycle of the collectives. Not only were the policies of the elite to be supported, "loyalist" volunteers were put in the position of having to ostracize other volunteers who expressed skepticism. The second point to be made about the collectives that "survived" is that they really were no longer collectives by the definition advanced in the beginning of this paper. That is, they had metamorphosed into bureaucratic institutions, stratified and fundamentally (though not explicitly) nonegalitarian. Of course, they were not constituted along the same lines as the traditional bureaucracy, with pyramid-shaped authority structures. The bureaucracy of the collectives tended to be two-tiered. Nevertheless, authority was anything but equally distributed. These organizations ended up in the unhappy position of claiming to be something they were not.

Summary and Conclusion

We have now come full circle in our examination of the life cycle of twelve urban workers' collectives. A close look at the histories of such organizations reveals that they are, in many cases, subject to a series of constraints which have the cumulative effect of encouraging the formation of hierarchies. Despite intentions to the contrary, many of the collectives evolved into bureaucratic institutions—the opposite of what they had intended.

The motivation behind this paper has been the desire to understand the nature of the pressures which fostered the growth of bureaucratic hierarchies in organizations formally and overtly committed to anti-

bureaucratic principles. For unlike Weber (1947), we do not accept the
dictum that bureaucratic organizations are necessarily the most advanced and efficient of human institutions. Implicit in the Weberian
position is the notion that bureaucracy develops because it is an
inherently superior structure for dealing with the exigencies of goal
attainment. However, as we have shown in the preceding sections of this
paper, the bureaucratization of the collectives cannot be attributed to
difficulties in the management of tasks. Rather, it was the dependence of
the collectives and their members upon external resources that provided
the initial push in the direction of hierarchy development. Thus, in
contrast to the quasi-Weberian position of *internally generated* bureaucracy, we take the view that incipient bureaucracy developed in these
organizations due to their relations with *external institutions*. This was
shown to be the case in those collectives that did not develop hierarchical
bureaucratic structures, but which successfully competed with bureaucratically organized businesses in providing goods and services to the
public. The crucial way in which they differed from their less successful
counterparts, the collectives which did bureaucratize, was in their
relationships to external institutions.

The accompanying figure presents a schematic representation of
the "stages" involved in hierarchy development within the collectives
and the consequences of bureaucratization for the continued existence of
these organizations. As the figure indicates, the collectives faced a rather
crucial decision early in their organizational development. They had to
determine whether or not to seek financial support from other more
powerful organizations. Those that were able to remain independent of
external funding sources were also able to remain egalitarian in their
authority structure. Those that had no alternative but to turn to
bureaucratic funding institutions started down the road to internal
hierarchy at this point. In short, the ethnographic histories of these
twelve collectives indicate that it was not the shortcomings of collective
decision making that led to the development of bureaucratic forms of
administration. Rather it was the increasing dependence on financial
support from the outside, the limited amount of that support, and the
internal ramifications of funding limitations that encouraged the
formation of anti-egalitarian forms of authority.

Once the decision had been made to enter the "granting game," the
collectives had to face an entirely different cultural milieu, one that
rejected the value system which they espoused. The larger society and its
institutions placed a positive value on hierarchy. The collectives had to
contend with this clash in normative orientations from a rather weak
position of financial dependency. Economic viability and cultural
evaluation were intertwined difficulties that the collectives had to face;

THE EVOLUTION OF HIERARCHY
IN URBAN WORKERS' COLLECTIVES

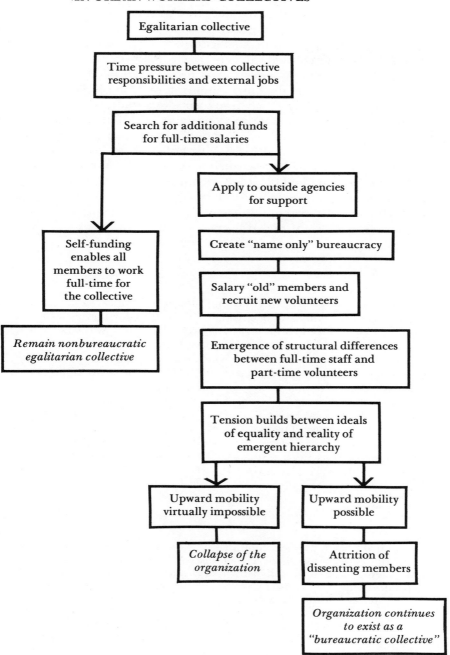

in many cases, as we have seen, "incipient bureaucratization" was the end result of this "culture contact."

The question arises as to whether or not such a development was inevitable. Were the cultural values of the late 1960s simply unworkable in practice and therefore doomed to failure in the case of the collectives? The fact that several of the organizations in this sample were able to persevere in their efforts to actualize their ideals leads us to reject this pessimistic view. However, the preponderance of collectives which did develop "incipient bureaucracies" should give us pause, for we have seen that even in the "survival" cases, many of these organizations could no longer be considered egalitarian. The moral of the story is, perhaps, that collectives are highly prone to bureaucratize in situations of dependency and scarce resources. The problems they faced were not so much a matter of inherent failures of egalitarian organizations; they were problems inherent in dependency relations.

Acknowledgments

An earlier version of this paper was presented at the annual meeting of the Pacific Sociological Association, April 1977. Support for the research was provided by U.S. Public Health Service grant GM 1207 to the Institute of Human Learning, University of California, Berkeley.

The ethnographic histories upon which this paper is based were collected by the author and by a group of students in the Department of Anthropology at the University of California, Berkeley. I would like to express my appreciation to the following individuals for their assistance: Mary Anton, Brett Carre, Emily Chao, Janet Davy, Brad Engle, Eric Fetzer, Robert Golden, Kevin Lew, David Moyce, William Novoa, Jr., Jo Ann Singer, Christine Sippl, and Ralph Troglione. While these students participated in a course project involving the ethnography of collectives, they are in no way responsible for the analysis presented in this paper. Any errors are the fault of the author.

Notes

1. Two of the three business collectives in this sample were able to forego soliciting external assistance, as indicated earlier. However, the one remaining was unable to collect sufficient capital from its membership to support its operating expenses. Thus, it was this organization that did apply to a bank for a loan. The story of bureaucratization that unfolds in the rest of this paper does not really apply to this organization, for like the other business collectives, it became self-supporting through retail trade, and its external dependency came to an end after it had repaid its initial loans. While this collective did have to establish a "name only" bureaucracy for the purpose of

soliciting these funds, the interference in its organizational structure never materialized as it did for the other nine collectives in the study.

2. One particularly popular source of temporary funding was the Comprehensive Employment and Training Act passed by the U.S. Congress. This legislation provided for temporary employment of individuals who had a previous history of unemployment. The funds were provided on a yearly basis and were thus only a short-term solution to the financial woes of the collectives. Nevertheless, they did prove very useful and in many cases were utilized as a needed supplement to grant funds.

References

Berger, B.
1971   *Looking for America.* Englewood Cliffs, N.J.: Prentice-Hall.
Blumberg, R.
1976   From the Fields of Revolution to the Laundries of Discontent. In L. Iglitzin and R. Ross (eds.), *Women in the World.* Oxford: ABC Cleo Press.
Chao, E.
1977   A Workers' Collective: A Personal View. Unpublished manuscript. Berkeley, Calif.
Collins, R.
1976   *Conflict Sociology.* New York: Academic Press.
Goffman, E.
1959   *The Presentation of Self in Everyday Life.* Garden City, N.Y.: Doubleday/Anchor.
Goulder, A.
1954   *Patterns of Industrial Bureaucracy.* New York: Free Press.
Grusky, O., and G. Miller
1970   *The Sociology of Organizations: Basic Studies.* New York: Free Press.
Lipset, S., M. Trow, and J. Coleman
1956   *Union Democracy.* Glencoe, Ill.: Free Press.
Michels, R.
1959   *Political Parties.* New York: Dover Press.
Powell, B.
1977   A Critical Look at the Center for Women's Studies and Services. Unpublished manuscript. San Diego, Calif.
Weber, M.
1947   *The Theory of Social and Economic Organization.* London: William Hodge.

10.

Bureaucratic Scholarship: The New Anthropology

BETTE DENICH

In 1928, Ruth Benedict wrote a letter to Margaret Mead (who was off on one of her field trips) describing the International Congress of Americanists of that year in the following terms:

> There was a lot of interest in my paper. . . . Kroeber's question was just, "how does the old man take a paper like that?" Edward said it was a good lecture and a good point, and Kidder came up to say it was illustrated just as much by the Pueblo art and material culture as by their religion. Wissler scowled through a great deal of it and I haven't seen him since; Elsie was speechless and rose to make all sorts of pointless addenda when she recovered her breath. Professor Danzel—the one from Hamburg, who's been staying with Gladys—said it was the most important paper of the Congress and agreed with work of his own; the same from Powdermaker. [Mead 1974: 36]

This passage illustrates the collegiality of anthropologists during the formative decades of the profession, when intellectual viewpoints and personalities blended indistinguishably into a whole way of life. Benedict's familiar references are to other leading figures of the time,[1] recognizable today as the pioneers of American anthropology (except, of course, for the visitor from Hamburg). Biographies of the earlier anthropologists lend insight into the flavor of the interpersonal and intellectual relationships of their era. In another example, Hortense Powdermaker recalled her classmates at the London School of Economics:

During my first year at LSE (1925) only three graduate students were in anthropology; the other two were E. E. Evans-Pritchard and Raymond Firth. Isaac Schapera came the second year and we were soon joined by Audrey Richards, Edith Clarke, the late Jack Driber, Camilla Wedgwood, and Gordon and Elizabeth Brown. Strong personal bonds developed between us and with Malinowski; it was a sort of family with the usual ambivalences. The atmosphere was in the European tradition: a master and his students, some in accord and others in opposition. [Powdermaker 1966: 36]

The biographies document how bonds between teachers and students, and among fellow students, were maintained over the spans of whole life careers. Dialogues were simultaneously scholarly and personal, friendships both collegial and intimate. Thus, Benedict's letter attaches ideas to definite personalities; the person and the thought are inseparable. "Papa" Franz Boas, Ruth Benedict, and Margaret Mead were in constant interchange from the time of Mead's undergraduate studies at Barnard until the deaths of Boas and Benedict. While Benedict and Mead continued to acknowledge the fatherly role of Boas as their professor, all three cooperated as peers in the advancement of their work at a time when anthropology was vigorous and widely influential among other social sciences. It is impressive to note the frequent acknowledgments by sociologists and psychologists of the influence of the anthropologists at Columbia during the 1930s and 1940s, when Boas, Benedict, and Mead were in the forefront of small community and personality research.

The purpose of the present paper is not to make a nostalgic journey into the past, but to use former times as a vantage point from which to view the present. I wish to show that, while anthropologists still idealize the traditions formed during the early decades of this century, the profession has undergone structural changes that have radically altered the nature of its intellectual life. Anthropologists today suffer from the same kind of disjuncture between image and reality that their field studies describe among cultures undergoing rapid change. The problem is to understand how relationships within anthropology are now structured, and the ways in which the structure affects scholarly work.

Numbers indicate the dimensions of the change. In 1901, Kroeber received the first Ph.D. awarded by Boas at Columbia, which was also the second Ph.D. in anthropology granted in the United States (Steward 1973: 6). By 1911, a total of six doctorates had been awarded at Columbia, including those to Robert Lowie, Edward Sapir, Alexander Goldenweiser, and Paul Radin. The profession at that time could hold its annual convention in one small meeting room (Murphy 1972: 11). By 1920, the Columbia department had awarded a total of fifty-one doctorates, while the Berkeley department, headed by Kroeber, awarded all of twenty-five degrees between 1908 and 1946. By contrast, in the single year 1973-74, Columbia awarded seventeen doctorates, and Berkeley twenty-eight. The total number of doctorates awarded nationally rose from twenty-four in 1947-48 to 409 in 1973-74, nearly a twenty-fold increase in twenty-five years. The small number of graduate departments rapidly proliferated during the 1950s and 1960s, to reach eighty-five departments granting the Ph.D. at present, of which seventy-five have actually produced at least one doctorate (D'Andrade et al. 1975: 768). Recent estimates indicate the total number of doctorates at somewhat over 2,600, and the total number of academic positions at something between 4,000 and 6,000 (D'Andrade et al. 1975: 760). Compared with dentists, or even historians, anthropologists are still a rare species. But compared with their own recent past, the rapid multiplication of anthropologists has been sufficient to burst the intimate small-scale circles of the past and to disperse them into the expanded number of spaces provided by the expanding institutions of the 1950s and 1960s. As the numbers have increased, the nature of the institutions has also changed, with effects on both the social context and intellectual content.

Max Weber (1947) defined bureaucratization in modern society as the replacement of traditional relationships, molded in feudalism, by the rational principles of capitalist enterprise, at a time when this process was most evident in the organization of the state and had not yet permeated all preexisting institutions, including universities and other arenas of intellectual activity. Social scientists have widely accepted the Weberian process as an inevitable, largely desirable prerequisite of modernization. As institutions become more bureaucratic, the social relations and behavior of the actors within them change in specified ways. In anthropology, it is possible to compare the nature of interpersonal relations of an earlier era with those of the present and to see that they follow the course of rationalization. Talcott Parsons (in Parsons et al. 1953) provided a vocabulary for analyzing the transition from traditional to rational behavior. The collegial relationships of earlier anthropologists fit perfectly into the boxes that Parsons would label "particularistic, affective, and functionally diffuse," all of which mean that a tie between specific individuals involves them as total personalities in a many-faceted relationship. The opposite categories identify bureaucratic relationships as "universalistic, instrumental, and functionally specific," meaning that relationships between individuals are defined by and limited to their roles in a single social context.

Although anthropology (along with some other scholarly fields) lagged in the rationalization of its structures, during the present generation the process has caught up with it. At this point, the personalistic past has been largely replaced by a universalistic present. Not to acknowledge this change is to operate as though ideas are independent of the social structure in which they are generated. Anthropologists still uphold the particularistic ideals inherited from the past and continue to imitate the forms of collegial dialogue described by Benedict and Powdermaker. For example, the symposia at professional meetings are designed as a meeting ground where colleagues with common interests can listen to and debate each other's ideas. The form endures, but it no longer presumes to represent anything beyond a four-hour session at which a number of papers on vaguely related topics are presented, with little if any cross-discussion. In contrast to the continuing relationships among the colleagues of former times, the relationships among today's symposia participants often begin and end with the session. It is a growing practice for organizers of symposia to advertise for papers on a general topic, and to select them solely on the basis of title and abstract, without prior acquaintance with or knowledge of the authors. When the papers are presented, the participants rarely recognize more than a few faces in the audience, and feel fortunate to receive a few comments on their efforts. Absent is the intensity of interest that Benedict's and Powdermaker's colleagues took in each other's work, the sharing that stimulated and rewarded their efforts.

The change in the nature of professional meetings has resulted from a gradual atrophy of personal ties, rather than from the conscious rejection of them. However, in many other aspects of professional life, personal ties are now considered illegitimate and have been deliberately replaced by universalistic practices, advocated and accepted in the interest of greater "fairness." In the area of job placement, personal networks have been replaced by the required advertising of openings, by search committees, and by submission and comparison of increasingly detailed *curricula vitae*. The replacement of the "old boy" by a committee to review applicants according to uniform criteria could serve as a textbook example of bureaucratization. Although it is common knowledge that the new rules are manipulated to provide a smokescreen for hiring practices that can still be as arbitrary as those of the past, the ideal represented by the new rules is not publicly questioned. Because universal standards seem to offer a way to evaluate people on their true merit, they are favored as the way to advance the quality of scholarship. However, a vital source of quality is sacrificed in the process.

In the former system, access to jobs and research funds was obtained through a unity of personal and intellectual relationships which linked elder and younger generations of scholars. Job openings were filled through recommendations on a personal basis, which maintained an intellectual bond on both sides between a senior professor, a former student, and a department in which the former student was placed in a job. A young professor thereby continued to be part of the scholarly network of graduate school years and kept up ties that spanned departmental and geographical boundaries. Today's new Ph.D.s (those who are lucky enough to find jobs at all) are usually hired on the basis of universalistic criteria, without previous relationship to anyone in their new department, and with letters of recommendation from professors who are likewise barely known to their employers. They thereby enter their departments as holders of bureaucratically defined jobs. Their success from that point then depends upon their ability to rise in the organizational structure of a college or university, invoking the typical methods required for advancement in corporations or in other impersonal organizations of this society. Scholarly credentials are established by quantity of publication, without consideration of the nature of ideas, as tenure committees—not qualified to evaluate the value of scholarship in a specific field—establish general standards. An extreme version of this trend is represented by one department that established a tenuring standard that equated one book with five articles, and granted more points to refereed journal articles than to articles in edited books. The outward forms of scholarship, exhibited in publication, are retained from the past, but the content is secondary, often to the point of irrelevance.

The scientific imagination thrives under circumstances that place the scientist in a social context that encourages creativity. Historians of science document how great discoveries were made by individual people relating to the scientific communities of their times and places. Thomas Kuhn (1962) has shown how a paradigm develops as a set of ideas among a network of scientists operating together in a social milieu. Therefore, the relationships among the individuals engaged in scientific work are essential to the quality of the work. It follows that a scholar divorced from an intellectual community is robbed of the environment necessary to the nourishment of creativity of the sort that is required for significant advances in knowledge. The discovery of the structure of DNA, for example, has been documented as a very human activity, involving many-faceted relationships among the individuals who cooperated and competed in making the breakthrough. The great leaps in twentieth-century nuclear physics are likewise traceable to interlinking circles of scientists spanning Europe and North America over several decades. In anthropology, the affective, long-term ties among the leading figures of the past were likewise intrinsic to their scientific output. The nature of communication among scholars directly affects their results. Spontaneous exchanges require an atmosphere of mutual trust and respect, established on a long-term basis. On the other hand, the formal presentations before largely anonymous audiences strive for intellectual closure and lack the kind of response which stimulates further thought and provokes the imagination to further leaps. Therefore, the loss of personal ties among anthropologists, the substitution of bureaucratic relationships, changes the nature of scholarship itself.

Preparation for a bureaucratically organized career now begins in graduate schools, where earlier generations began to form lifelong bonds with professors and with fellow students. The question "under whom did you work at (Harvard, Chicago . . .)" implied an important bond and theoretical influence, the basis for intellectual "schools" or traditions centering on leading professors and their former students. Today, the question is still asked, but rings hollow when the dissertation sponsor performs a very specific function and the student often works with a committee rather than an individual. Even a close professor-student relationship tends to diminish as the professor necessarily shifts attention to the sizable crop of current students and allows relationships with former students to lapse. From the student viewpoint, the relationship is likewise time-bounded and instrumental. I was amazed when some of the students I helped to prepare for their Ph.D. exams and field research never bothered to drop by or look me up when they returned from their faraway adventures. Rather then trying to maintain an intellectual tie, such students accurately gauge career realities which place little value on protracting relationships with professors not offering obvious future rewards.

Ties among fellow students have undergone a similar change. Student years are significant as the last phase before full adulthood, and are a time when close ties readily form among a group undergoing common experiences and ordeals. In the past, intellectual comradeship with fellow students continued throughout a scholar's lifetime to provide a core of associates, collaborators, and drinking pals with whom a free give-and-take was possible. Recent students reflect the values of the wider society, which is oriented toward preparing highly mobile organization men who follow their career paths as individuals, unfettered by permanent attachments. Graduate students are trained to maximize career opportunities and to slough off personal bonds as they move on. In anthropology, an important transition occurs when the student, returning from predoctoral field research, finds that there is no context for sharing experiences and ideas with anyone except the dissertation sponsor, with whom formal conferences are held. From the collective anxiety of student life, to the lonely quest of fieldwork, to the enforced isolation of writing the dissertation, the student is prepared to embark on an individual career, leaving behind the old school and all that went with it. A myth of friendship among past fellow students, renewed each year at the annual meeting, is based on an ever-receding past, rather than on ongoing intellectual and personal communication. The finality of the loss consists in the lack of substitutes, because the faculty experience does not provide ties of the same sort. Anthropologists of recent vintages find themselves with few, if any, colleagues with whom they enjoy the kind of personalistic relationships needed in a real scientific community.

As communication is removed from face-to-face primary networks, scholars rely on the printed word. The exchange is thus filtered through journal articles and academic monographs which have adopted standardized formats, discouraging individual variations in writing styles. Anthropological writing that possesses literary value is so rare that the exceptions stand out. Graduate schools discourage the literary talents that some students retain through their undergraduate studies and channel all writing into a pattern that is more rigid than rigorous. The journals exert the same influence, rarely selecting articles for publication that vary from a narrow range of expression. Research funds are likewise granted on the basis of research proposals that follow standardized formats, amenable to evaluation according to universalistic criteria. The anonymous reviewers of journal articles and research proposals judge how well the author succeeds in fitting the mold. The anonymity principle has recently expanded to include the authorship of articles submitted to journal reviewers, who are asked to judge the article apart from its author, upholding the universalistic premise that the personal attributes of scholars are irrelevant to their work.

The rationalization process continues inescapably. As I typed this article, I received a request from a government funding agency to correct a computer printout of information about me as a reviewer, to aid them in their transfer of records from a manual to an automated system. Now a computer will provide the link between anthropologists applying for grants and those reviewing the applications.

As the journals and other publications supplant informal dialogue as the primary medium of communication, it is important to question how the ideas expressed are affected. As authors strive to meet universal, anonymous standards, they shape their work to conform to the legitimized norms and avoid subjects and writing styles that stand out from the crowd. The controversial, the highly original, have no place. But ideas have never developed through consensus, and the clash between rival paradigms is essential to the advancement of scientific knowledge. What, then, is the effect of conformity to the requirements of anonymous, interchangeable evaluators? One effect is the constricted range of theoretical debate. Over the years, verbal duels rage and wane over such seemingly innocuous topics as the "image of limited good" and the "substantivist-formalist controversy," which are phrased in terms meaningless to the uninitiated. The intellectual passion unleashed in these debates is real, but it comes from underlying conflicts in basic principles that rarely, if ever, appear on the surface. Opposing sides rally in response to cues and innuendoes, while significant theoretical questions are relegated to the space between the lines. A clear statement of deeper levels of debate would violate the accepted mode of discourse, face rejection by reviewers for journals and publishers, and subject its author to scorn or, at best, notoriety.

Because the forms of discourse muffle the viewpoints under debate, there is a direct connection between the medium of communication, the ideas expressed, and the thinking process itself. When a science does not address basic questions, but carries out routinized research leading to standardized research reports, it may be in a phase that Thomas Kuhn calls "normal science," in which a dominant paradigm is generally accepted by the community of scientists. If anthropology is now in a period of "normal science," then what theoretical consensus has been reached? The question is unanswerable within the present range of acceptable discourse.

Although the intellectual perspective of anthropology places it outside the boundaries of a single culture, the field itself cannot escape the social structures of which its practitioners are actually part. At its base, anthropology is a profession from which people make a living, subject to the same pressures as any other occupational category. To understand the reasons for change, it is necessary to look at the sources and distribution of the material resources that support its activities and provide its members with their livelihood. The present sources of financial support for anthropology can be understood in perspective when compared with the funding sources of the past. Kroeber's biography describes how, in the early years of this century, he raised research funds and supported his own salary as museum director through personal appeals to wealthy San Francisco patrons. Having obtained funds in this manner, he could allocate them according to his own judgment regarding the proper direction for anthropology in California. Through personal persuasion, he had to satisfy his benefactors that his work deserved their continued support. This funding method fit the realities of turn-of-the-century America, when new industrial wealth was controlled by individual owners, who dispensed their largesse according to their particular fancies.

During the following decades, the development of corporate

capitalism has followed its path toward large-scale, increasingly rational organization, in which variable personal qualities are eliminated. This process has taken primary hold in the economy, where many free, competing enterprises have been replaced by a small number of vast, diversified corporations that divide up each field of endeavor and extend themselves over many different forms of activity. The modern corporation seeks anonymity, hiding the consolidation of ownership behind the enduring trade names which formerly identified independent companies owned by the recognizable entrepreneurs of the early industrial era—who were also the individual patrons of arts and sciences.

The corporate form of organization eventually encompassed universities and other havens of scholarship where specialists in esoteric fields stayed outside the mainstream of society. The expansion in the number of anthropologists through the 1950s and 1960s was financed by governmental agencies and private foundations as part of a general policy that absorbed educational institutions into the expanding corporate sphere. The seduction of individual scholars and academic departments was easily achieved as they found themselves in line for rich new sources of funds to underwrite the expansion of departments and worldwide research on a far grander scale than the academicians of the past had imagined possible. To anthropologists whose previous research was financed largely by small private grants, the new funds glittered indeed. To get them, they had only to learn to formulate research problems in categories established by the foundations and government agencies in the bureaucratic mold of rational procedure. The research proposal, and the thought processes required to successfully fulfill it, therefore superseded the older, more individual approaches to the pursuit of knowledge. The changes in anthropology constituted just one small part of a wider process leading to the present situation in which government funding, tax-exempt foundations, and grant applications permeate all levels of American society, with their abstract formulas to which applications must either conform or die.

The bureaucratization of research finance has a direct effect on what scientists think about as well as on the ways that they think. Funding agencies decide which problem areas merit their support and reward those scholars whose research fits the approved categories. The impetus for new directions that formerly came from collegial discussion now comes from directives issued by the agencies. There is a bonus to those who anticipate trends and therefore get first chance at monies allocated to new research areas. In the spirit of objectivity, proposals are reviewed by anonymous committees of fellow scientists, another instance in which the collegial tie is sacrificed to anonymity, with little sense that something is lost in the process. The personal ties from which past anthropologists derived their intellectual sustenance have diminished, almost unnoticed, to the point of near-extinction.

Bureaucracy is an aspect of modern society with which all citizens have direct experience. Rationality—the achievement of predictable results from standardized inputs—is highly functional to the smooth operation of the large-scale organizations of an industrial society. In academic fields, the rise of universalistic values is associated with a desire for greater equality and fairness, and has been especially favored as a device to increase the chance of women and minorities to enter ranks previously monopolized by white males of particular backgrounds. However, rules that should ensure rewards based on pure merit, rather than on other personal attributes, are easily circumvented as long as white male applicants are available. In the meantime, the restructuring of relationships that has occurred in the name of equality has taken hold as a change that cannot be readily bypassed by individuals who desire the collegiality of the past. The significance of the change for anthropology as an intellectual discipline is not so much in the loss of a lifestyle that some people found congenial, but in the effect on the ideas and the written works which make up the contribution of contemporary anthropology to human knowledge. The processes whereby ideas are generated affect the nature of the ideas. Bureaucratic processes lead to predictable, routinized results in scholarship, just as surely as they do in post offices.

Note

1. The anthropologists referred to by Benedict are: Franz Boas (the "old man"), Alfred Kroeber, Edward Sapir, Alfred Kidder, Clark Wissler, Elsie Clews Parsons, Gladys Reichard, and Hortense Powdermaker.

Acknowledgment

An earlier version of this paper entitled "On the Bureaucratization of Scholarship in American Anthropology" was published in volume 2 of the journal *Dialectical Anthropology* (1977).

References

D'Andrade, Roy et al.
    1975   Academic Opportunity in Anthropology 1974–90. *American Anthropologist* 77: 753–73.

Kuhn, Thomas
    1962   *The Structure of Scientific Revolutions*. Chicago: University of
            Chicago Press.
Mead, Margaret
    1974   *Ruth Benedict*. New York: Columbia University Press.
Murphy, Robert F.
    1972   *Robert Lowie*. New York: Columbia University Press.
Parsons, Talcott, R. F. Bales, and E. A. Shils
    1953   *Working Papers in the Theory of Action*. Glencoe, Ill.: Free Press.
Powdermaker, Hortense
    1966   *Stranger and Friend*. New York: Norton.
Steward, Julian
    1973   *Alfred Kroeber*. New York: Columbia University Press.
Weber, Max
    1947   *The Theory of Social and Economic Organization*. New York:
            Oxford University Press.

Notes on the Contributors

Gerald M. Britan is an Assistant Professor of Anthropology and Urban Affairs at Northwestern University. He received his Ph.D. in anthropology in 1974 from Columbia University, and has conducted research on social and economic change in rural Newfoundland, on bureaucratic reform in Washington, D.C., and on the planning and evaluation of numerous social service and social action programs. His current interests focus on innovation, directed social change, evaluation research, and the anthropology of formal organizations. His major publications include: *Public Policy and Innovation, The Schooner Fishermen* (forthcoming), "Environment and Choice in Rapid Social Change" (with B. Denich), "Modernization of the North Atlantic Coast," "The Place of Anthropology in Program Evaluation," "Experimental and Contextual Models of Program Evaluation," and "Systems Theory in Anthropology" (with M. Rodin and K. Michaelson).

Michael Chibnik, Assistant Professor of Anthropology at the University of Iowa, received a Ph.D. in anthropology in 1975 from Columbia University. He has studied and written about agricultural decision-making in rural Belize, the social impact of computerized technology in North American business offices, and consumer behavior in Hawaii.

Ronald Cohen is a Professor of Anthropology and Political Science at Northwestern University. He has carried out anthropological fieldwork in Africa, northern Canada, and the United States, and has been a major consultant in the planning and design of Nigeria's new capital city of Abuja. His major publications include: *The Kanuri of Bornu, From Tribe to Nation in Africa* (edited with John Middleton), *Dominance and Defiance, Handbook of Method in Cultural Anthropology* (edited with R. Naroll), and *Origins of the State* (edited with E. R. Service).

Bette Denich received her Ph.D. in anthropology from the University of California, Berkeley, in 1970. She has taught at Columbia University, and is currently working as an independent anthropological consultant. Her interests include modernization, migration, urbanization, and the changing status of women, especially in Eastern Europe. More recently, she has focused on energy and environmental problems in the United States. Her major publications include: "Sex and Power in the Balkans," "Environment and Choice in Rapid Social Change" (with G. Britan), "Urbanization and Women's Roles in the Yugoslav Revolution," "Sources of Leadership in the Yugoslav Revolution," "Women, Work and Power in Modern Yugoslavia," and "Migration and Network Manipulation in Yugoslavia."

Laura Nader is a Professor of Anthropology at the University of California, Berkeley. She has been a fellow at the Institute for Advanced Study in the Behavioral Sciences in Palo Alto, and at the Woodrow Wilson Center in Washington, D.C. She received her Ph.D. in anthropology from Radcliffe in 1961. Professor Nader has conducted research among the Zapotec Indians in Oaxaca, Mexico, among the Shia Moslems in south Lebanon, and on a range of policy issues in the United States. Her major interests are legal anthropology and the social impact of America's political and corporate elites. Some of Professor Nader's major publications are: *Talea and Juquila, The Ethnography of Law, Law in Culture and Society, The Disputing Process*, and *No Access to Law: Alternatives to the American Judicial System*. Professor Nader's most recent research focuses on issues of energy and the law, and her writings on this subject include: "Human Dimensions of Energy Research," "Energy and the Quality of Life," and *Energy Choices in Democratic Society*.

Katherine Newman received her Ph.D. in anthropology at the University of California, Berkeley, in 1979. She has been interested in ethnographic studies of formal organizations for a number of years, and has pursued research in several bureaucratic settings, including the sales office of a major corporation, paramedical organizations in the military, and various state agencies. She is a member of the faculty of the Jurisprudence and Social Policy Program in the School of Law. She is conducting research on regulatory agencies and conflict management.

Charles B. Rosen received his Ph.D. in anthropology from the University of Chicago in 1974. Prior to that, he spent four years in Ethiopia, the last two devoted to anthropological fieldwork. His work concentrated on the local politics and administration of empirial Ethiopia. Currently his interests center on religion, and he is exploring an anthropological approach to understanding Orthodox Judaism in America and in Israel. He has written a number of articles on the politics of Tigray, Ethiopia, and has a book in preparation, *Warring with Words: Patterns of Political Activity in a Northern Ethiopian Town*.

Helen B. Schwartzman is a Senior Research Scientist at the Institute for Juvenile Research, Illinois Mental Health Institutes. She received her Ph.D. in anthropology in 1973 from Northwestern University. Her research interests include the study of bureaucratic cultures in American society, the impact of formal organizations on children and families, relationships between work and play in industrialized and nonindustrialized societies, and the analysis of children's play communication. Her publications include: *Transformations: The Anthropology of Children's Play, Play and Culture*, and "Culture Conflict in a Community Mental Health Center" (with A. W. Kneifel and M. S. Krause).

Martin King Whyte received his M.A. from Harvard University in Russian area studies in 1966, his Ph.D. from Harvard in sociology in 1971; he is currently Associate Professor and Associate Chairman of the Department of Sociology, University of Michigan. His publications include: *Small Groups and Political Rituals in China, The Status of Women in Preindustrial Societies, Village and Family in Contemporary China*, and "Revolutionary Social Change and Patrilocal Residence in China." Professor Whyte is a specialist in comparative sociology, family sociology, and the sociological study of China. He has lived in Hong Kong for three years, and has visited China on three separate occasions. His current research focuses on urban social structure and neighborhood organization in contemporary China.

Index